PRAISE FOR *ENCORE*

"Mr. Freedman, founder and chief executive of Civic Ventures, a San Francisco nonprofit, writes about 'encore careers'—jobs in later life that involve 'continued income, new meaning, and [a] significant contribution to the greater good.' The five 'mini' autobiographies of people who have embraced such careers are alone worth the price of admission."
—*Wall Street Journal*

"Freedman provides concrete steps to finding a meaningful new job, and he profiles people who have succeeded in their second acts."
—Best Books, Planning a Second Career,
U.S. News and World Report

"Another book by Freedman in 2002 . . . foresaw many of the trends others regurgitate now. His latest work may be just as visionary."
—*Tribune Media Services*

"Read it: Take the weekend to consider what you want to do in the second half of your life." —*Arizona Republic*

"Through his thoughtful and undeniable thesis, Freedman constructs a utopian working life filled with possibility. . . . I give the book four full cups of fair trade, organic coffee."
—*Training and Development Magazine*

"Freedman persuasively argues that later years can offer freedom to work in more flexible, meaningful ways, rather than only a time to be free from work." —*Minneapolis Star Tribune*

"In this timely and important book, Marc Freedman overturns the conventional wisdom about work, retirement, and even the American Dream. If you're a boomer—especially if you're a boomer running for president—put *Encore* at the top of your reading pile. This is the rare book that can change the national conversation."
—Daniel H. Pink, author of *A Whole New Mind*
and *Free Agent Nation*

"Many millions of maturing baby boomers will thank Marc Freedman for this warm, wise, compelling, and hopeful book. *Encore* contains both eye-opening stories and important guidance for policymakers, to ensure that people can continue to make meaningful contributions throughout their longer lifetimes."

—Rosabeth Moss Kanter, Harvard Business School, and best-selling author of *Confidence: How Winning Streaks and Losing Streaks Begin and End*

"Sixty-four million baby boomers—40 percent of the current American work force—will reach retirement age by 2010. They will be the largest, healthiest, longest-living, and best-educated generation in American history—to do what? Golf? Soldier on in old jobs? Or, adopting Freedman's inspirational idea, use their gifts and experience to build a better world through an 'encore career.' Featuring a series of moving life stories, Freedman makes a convincing case for a brilliant idea whose time has come."

—Arlie Hochschild, University of California, Berkeley, and author of *The Time Bind: When Work Is Home and Home Is Work* and *The Commercialization of Intimate Life*

"Marc Freedman is a plausible candidate for secular sainthood. For more than a decade this gifted social activist has worked toward an America in which aging boomers help themselves and their communities through community service—what he calls 'the encore society.' This well-crafted book spells out the latest development of his thesis and illustrates it with compelling personal stories."

—Robert D. Putnam, Kennedy School of Government, Harvard University, and author of *Bowling Alone: The Collapse and Revival of American Community*

"Every movement needs a visionary, and baby boomers eager for meaningful second acts are lucky to have Marc Freedman. This remarkable book is as inspiring as it is important, as compelling for individuals as it is for society."

—Sherry Lansing, CEO, Sherry Lansing Foundation, former chairman of Paramount Pictures

"In *Encore*, Marc Freedman provocatively confronts the impact baby boomers will have on society as they age. This is a very important book for the public, for program planners, and for policymakers alike."

—Gene D. Cohen, MD, PhD, George Washington University, and author of *The Mature Mind: The Positive Power of the Aging Brain*

Encore

Encore

.

Finding Work That Matters
in the
Second Half of Life

.

MARC FREEDMAN

with Photographs by Alex Harris

PUBLICAFFAIRS
New York

Text design and composition by Jenny Dossin

A CATALOGING-IN-PUBLICATION RECORD FOR THIS BOOK IS AVAILABLE
FROM THE LIBRARY OF CONGRESS.
HC: ISBN-13: 978-1-58648-483-5; ISBN-10: 1-58648-483-4
PB: ISBN-13: 978-1-58648-634-1

10 9 8 7 6 5 4 3 2

For Leslie, Gabriel, and Levi,
with love and appreciation

CONTENTS

The pitcher cries for water to carry
and a person for work that is real.

MARGE PIERCY, "TO BE OF USE"

Encore

CHAPTER ONE

The Freedom to Work

The year is 2030.

The youngest baby boomers are midway through their sixties and starting to claim their Social Security benefits. And none too soon, since the coffers are nearly empty. As many boomers say with only a touch of irony, at least we got ours.

The fittest boomers still boast that eighty is the new sixty, but the rest of the country has gotten tired of footing the bill for their lengthy retirement. After a seemingly endless run, America is ready for the baby boom generation to finally get off the stage.

With more than one in four Americans over sixty in this future society, generational conflicts abound. Walkers outnumber strollers; nursing homes proliferate while schools close. The millennial generation, now mostly in their thirties and forties, have taken "extreme working" to new heights, pulling extra shifts to support not only truly needy children and the elderly, but also a vast cohort of "greedy geezers" spending one-third of their lives on subsidized vacation. California, with the nation's largest population of individuals over sixty, is the first to experience the ethnic division exacerbated by the aging crisis, as an older, largely white minority confronts a younger and largely Latino majority in the annual budget wars.

The nation owes a debt to the boomers, in the form of an intractable deficit pushing the country ever closer to default. Spending on boomers' pensions and health care has replaced nearly all investments in the nation's future. Not only children, but the environment and the economy are suffering from these lost opportunities. America, like its swelling population of pensioners, is visibly and painfully well past its prime.

As the 2032 presidential election nears, boomer political power is finally on the wane. But the generation's legacy is assured. Boomers will be remembered as a self-absorbed, self-serving horde of overindulgers who used their votes and their dollars to push their own interests to the forefront, posterity be damned.

.   .   .

Now imagine a different scenario.

It's still 2030. The boomers are indeed starting to leave the stage. But their encore has been a rousing one and the legacy they leave is far different.

The hysterical predictions of academic economists and assorted policy experts that once dominated discussion about the inevitable demographic trends have proven false. Few even remember concerns that the nation was headed to hell in a handbasket because of the huge population of "retiring" boomers. The feared "Gray2K" was a nonevent, just like Y2K before it.

Instead, there is a palpable sense of progress. Longevity, demography, human development, generational experience, fiscal imperatives, labor market dictates, and the particular historical moment combined to lead boomers to contribute longer and to use their education and experience in areas with jobs to offer, deeper meaning to confer, and broader social purposes to fulfill.

Faced with the practical necessity of extended working lives, boomers have made it a virtue, getting busy on their next chapters, second acts, or Careers 2.0. Some of the ills that seemed intractable at the beginning of the twenty-first century are fading, and others that appeared only to be worsening have made a 180° turn—all thanks to boomer labor power, now known as the "experience dividend."

Now, nearly everyone looks forward to an encore career. The oldest members of the millennial generation, entering their fifties, are getting ready for their own second acts, and younger people clamor for "purpose-driven jobs" in the same way earlier generations embraced early retirement. The goal now is to be able to stop climbing the ladder and start making a difference, to trade money for meaning, to have the latitude to work on things that matter most.

Other nations, aging even faster than the United States, have imported the model as well. And no wonder, given the results:

- The boomers now function as the backbone of education, health care, nonprofits, the government, and other sectors essential to national well-being. This group is serving as the glue of society in much the way women carried a whole set of caring professions in the first half of the twentieth century. And the windfall has not just been in numbers and experience. Second-stage social entrepreneurship and innovation is being spearheaded by individuals bringing the accumulated skills from the first half of working life to the higher goals of their second acts.

- New rites of passage have emerged. The "gap year . . . or two" sabbatical between midlife and the encore career now fulfills at least some of the old fantasy of freedom in retirement, but it also serves as the transition to an encore. What is now known as "retirement" generally takes place in people's mid-seventies, after their encore careers. Many work even longer. Social Security, far from being bankrupt, runs a modest surplus and is able to support the truly dependent, including the one-fifth of the older population—a number that continues to decline—who retire on disability by the age of sixty-five.

- Whole new industries and institutions service boomers on the path to new purpose. Meanwhile, financial services firms and other businesses have found considerable profit in helping individuals plan for their encore phase of work and contribution. Rather than saving in midlife to finance outright retirement in their late fifties or early to mid-sixties, with no income from work, people save in their middle years to buy an extra measure of freedom in their second half of work—for a time when they can swap income for impact.

- Spurred by enlightened public policy, encore careers provide a second chance at upward mobility for individuals from the less affluent end of the socioeconomic spectrum. New skills and increased education open new doors, reflecting the emerging reality that this chapter of work is not only about using your experience but also about acquiring new know-how. The "experience economy" takes on an entirely new meaning in the process.

- As continued engagement and purpose serve as a fitness program for the body and the brain, life expectancy likewise continues to climb. More and more people seem to have a second, and even a third, "encore," as their health and energy hold out well into their eighties and nineties.

Demography turns out not to be destiny after all, at least not in the way pundits once proclaimed. But those prognosticators were right in another way. The present situation feels inevitable, as natural as the oxygen in the air. The suggestion that it wasn't always this way brings a quick response from those in this society of 2030: Not possible! We'd never survive writing off the most experienced segment of the population in the middle of their productive years. Haven't things always been this way?

As the 2032 election approaches, political power is indeed passing to a new generation. But the boomer legacy is assured: A generation that set out to change the world surely did, by changing the way the world thought about the purpose of work and the definition of success, and by rolling up its sleeves and doing the work that needed to be done.

A New Stage of Work

The more appealing view from 2030 might sound like a utopian fantasy. After all, most of the economic forecasts and policy predictions today point in the opposite direction; the prospect of a boomer-driven downward spiral comes directly from the congressional testimony of no less an authority than Federal Reserve Board Chairman Ben Bernanke—echoing his predecessor, Alan Greenspan (who retired at the age of seventy-nine).

Of course, worst-case scenarios of hand-wringing politicians and experts do sometimes come to pass. However, nearly all the dire scenarios that have become such a prominent part of the intellectual and policy landscape contain a simple, central fallacy: They take retirement as we've known it as a given and a constant. A relatively recent social institution is treated as an eternal verity, and all planning revolves around it.

The predictors of doom jam together the new *numbers*, the demographic reality of a vast flood of boomers moving through their sixties and beyond, with the old *lifestyle*, a static conception of future behavior based on the leisure-driven retirement that was the hallmark of the past. This is scenario building through the rearview mirror.

The absurdity of this assumption is apparent in an advertisement from Allstate, aimed at the boomers and touting their financial planning services. The advertisement starts with a clever line that is true enough: "The generation that wouldn't trust anyone over 30," the banner begins, "never planned on a 30-year retirement."

A timeline shows six marks stretching from life's beginning to its end. The left half offers caricatures of the same person at birth, childhood, and adulthood. The right half provides three more depictions of the man, slowly aging through retirement, retirement, retirement. He repeatedly checks his watch with increasing frustration as his beard grows ever longer and endless retirement defines the second half of life.

Then Allstate reverts to convention. The ad posits boomers' greatest fear: "living to see the well run dry." The point: Dramatic extension of life expectancy in the United States requires an equally dramatic investment in one's own retirement savings. After all, how else can you sustain thirty years, half of one's adulthood, outside the working life? The ad drives to its punch line: "Let's save retirement by saving for retirement. That's Allstate's stand."

But who looks forward to endless retirement, thirty years of R & R? More to the point: who can afford it—even with the most diligent savings plan? Allstate's vision, like the Golden Years version of retirement that reigned over the past half century, is already obsolete. Stretched from a sensible and justified period of leisure and relaxation into a phase as long as midlife in duration, retirement, once a powerful version of the American dream, has been distorted into something that no longer works for most individuals—or for the nation.

Still, dreams die hard, especially when so much money and so much inertia are tied up in the enterprise. Until a new dream emerges.

The emerging reality looks like this: Retirement as we have known it is in the midst of being displaced as the central institution of the second half of life. It is being supplanted by a new stage of life opening up between the end of midlife and the arrival of true old age, a period that essentially amounts to the second half of life, at least adult life. And that's just half of it: The new phase under development is every bit as much a new stage of *work*.

We now know that baby boomers are going to work longer than their parents did, whether they have to or want to, or most likely of all, are propelled to extended working lives by some combination of the two. Four out of five boomers consistently tell researchers that they expect to work well into what used to be known as the retirement years.

The movement of millions of these individuals into a new phase of work constitutes one of the most significant transformations in work this country has witnessed since millions of women broke through to new roles in the labor market, roles that had been off-limits to their mothers' generation. (Of course, many of these new pioneers are the same women who broke down those earlier barriers and are poised to transform work one more time.) And much like the movement of women into the workplace, boomers' extended stay on the job is likely to have reverberations for all generations and for the very nature of work in America.

The shift toward much longer working lives is already underway. Since the mid-1990s, this inclination has emerged as a significant new pattern, reversing a decades-long trend toward earlier and earlier retirement. Between 2003 and 2005, workers over 55 comprised the fastest-growing group of employees in the country, with employment among these older workers growing 10.5 percent. The group with the second-fastest growth rate, workers 45–54 years old, grew by 4.1 percent. The number of workers between 25 and 44 actually declined.

This pattern is likely to continue, and—handled right—it should continue. Longer working lives bring with them many potential benefits for both individuals and society, and dramatically improve the fiscal picture of a much grayer nation. Yet for all this agreement, we remain in an awkward transitional phase. The old norm for this period is in rapid eclipse, yet the new dream remains to be shaped. Crosscurrents and contradictions leave a landscape that makes little sense, including a language riddled with oxymorons ("retirement jobs," the "young-old," and the like).

Indeed, many of the most important questions about this vast and important phenomenon remain not only unanswered but rarely asked. What kind of work are these individuals hoping to do? What do they want to accomplish through work in this new stage? Are they in any position to make these contributions? Are employers ready to hire them? Perhaps most important of all, what kind of contribution do we need them to make? Is there any alignment between individual desires, labor market opportunity, and society's needs—or are we careening toward "the big disconnect," as Glenn Ruffenbach of the *Wall Street Journal* posits?

In this vacuum, a model of work has come to the forefront—bridge jobs in the retail sector—in essence, substituting the Wal-Mart Years for the Golden Years. There's something to be said for bridge jobs as one option available to aging boomers, especially in positions offering benefits; however, we are in danger of this route becoming the default arrangement. That would be great news for retailers' bottom line, but it hardly constitutes the highest and best use of a generation—especially the largest, healthiest, longest-lived, and best-educated generation in American history.

This book tells the story of an incipient movement of individuals who embody a powerful alternative, who are living out a distinct and compelling vision of work in the second half of life, one built around the dream of an "encore career" at the intersection of continued income, new meaning, and significant contribution to the greater good. It is a dream with the potential to work at once for individuals, for employers, for our nation's fiscal health, and for society more broadly.

A recent advertisement from the Principal Financial Group brings the choice of these individuals into sharp relief. The question above a photograph of an athletic, sixty-something woman wearing a wet suit, toting a surfboard, beaming with satisfaction, and heading for the shore: "Why do we work?" Principal answers it: "For the freedom that a secure retirement brings." That is, for the freedom from work, the liberation from labor. The piece concludes with the assurance: "We understand what you're working for"—essentially, to not work anymore.

The encore career pioneers are heading toward a different shore. They have asked the same question, "Why work?" but they have come to a different conclusion. Instead of the freedom *from* work, they are searching for the freedom *to* work; instead of saving for a "secure retirement," they are underwriting an encore career. Instead of accepting the notion of a career as an arc that rises in youth, peaks in midlife, and declines into retirement, they are charting a new trajectory— one that for many will reach its apex of meaning and impact when others in past generations headed for the sidelines.

Their vision of work in the new stage of life amounts to more than a recipe for averting the apocalyptic scenarios of generational warfare and social collapse associated with a much older nation. It brings with it the opportunity to do better than simply muddle through a radical reshuffling of the age distribution, but to break through to a new era of individual and social renewal, to ride the wave of longevity and health toward a future that works better for all generations.

Finding Work That Matters

In her quiet way, Beverly Ryder is used to being among the first. She was part of the first large entering class of African American students at Stanford University. She was part of the first significant group of women to get MBAs and move in meaningful numbers into new management positions in the corporate world. Now she is among the first wave of baby boomers to enter a new stage of life and work, looking for more. But for Ryder the road ahead is not just about being a pioneer. It is a return to an earlier promise.

Ryder grew up in Baldwin Hills in Los Angeles's postwar black middle class, in a family of distinguished professionals. In 1968, she graduated from Susan Miller Dorsey High, and remembers herself as "a typical middle-class kid, using public institutions." By the time she headed to Stanford that fall, Martin Luther King Jr. and Robert Kennedy had been assassinated. Riots had flared in urban areas around the country. The Black Power movement gained worldwide attention when John Carlos and Tommy Smith took the medal stand at the Mexico City Olympics. In May, French students had stormed the barricades in Paris. At Stanford, nicknamed "The Farm" for its bucolic environment, Ryder remembers students throwing a mailbox through President Richard Lyman's window and city police coming onto campus for the first time to restore order.

Ryder's father, one of the few black aeronautical engineers working in the defense industry, had a security clearance and warned her not to get arrested. Ryder laughs about that now. "I was a petition signer, not a bomb thrower," she says. "I'm one of those people who really believes that to make change you have to do it from both sides—the outside and the inside. You need external pressure, but I'm not an external radical. Hopefully if you are in the right place, you can make that change from the inside."

Ryder set out to be that inside person. She majored in economics, went on to get an MBA at the University of

Chicago, and, determined to learn how the business world worked, she took her first job at Citibank in New York, working during the legendary Walter Wriston era. She had spent sixteen years there helping to run the bank's corporate finance division when she was recruited by Edison International, the major gas and electric utility and parent of Southern California Edison. The assignment: Move back to L.A. and assume a senior management role.

Returning to her hometown in the early 1990s, Ryder found that L.A.'s once-accomplished schools were among the sorest spots in California's ravaged educational system. Today, fewer than half of L.A.'s high school students graduate, with more than 30,000 dropping out every year. More than half of the city's forty-six high schools are designated as "failing."

"I grew up in Los Angeles. I went to public schools here. The L.A. schools helped make me what I am," Ryder says. "Why can't that be done today?" The question nagged at Ryder as she got more involved in her old hometown, through her work at the utility, volunteering with civic associations, and serving on nonprofit boards, including the United Way of Greater Los Angeles, the Los Angeles Urban League, and the Los Angeles Conservation Corps.

After a dozen years at Edison, during which she became a corporate officer, Ryder worked with Edison to make her a "loaned executive" to the social sector. She talked to many groups, but the pull of public education was powerful. In 2005, Ryder went to work at Crenshaw High, a school with

2,700 students in southwest Los Angeles, just two miles from her alma mater. There, she helped launch a model program to build connections between the school and the local community, including local businesses. She sometimes worked fifteen-hour days, arriving at daybreak to meet with the principal, going to community meetings late into the night. There were times when she felt exhausted—"I don't want to live on four hours of sleep a night"—but she also became steadily more determined to make change.

Ryder began working with the Los Angeles Unified School District, helping to create a new office to shape the

Beverly Ryder

many partnerships the district and individual schools were forming with private companies and outside groups. And, taking the next step, in 2006 she applied to and was accepted by the Broad Academy, a ten-month program preparing leaders from the private sector, the military, and the non-profit world to become urban public school superintendents.

Beverly Ryder's route back to her home community is as much generational as geographic—the story of one individual's socially conscious second act in formation, as well as the journey of a baby boomer who came of age in the late 1960s, left college determined to create a better world, and is now focusing on those goals with renewed determination.

When Ryder talks with her associates, she hears many of them contemplating a similar trajectory, yearning for greater meaning through work, contemplating new priorities to focus on what matters most. "They tell me, 'I have done whatever I'm going to do from a financial standpoint. I don't need all the stuff that I thought I needed before. I can do this work at a lesser salary now than I could ten years ago when I had to put my kids through school.'"

One of her friends, a former businessman, has become a math teacher at Crenshaw High. "He's not Bill Gates," Ryder quips. He still needs to make a salary, but he doesn't need to make as much as he did in years past. That has meant a new freedom, not to stop working but to work in a way that's more aligned with his shifting priorities.

When that renegotiation begins—between money and meaning, between practicalities and purpose, between the

world today and the one we'd like to leave for future generations—a realization takes hold that there may be one more
chance to return to an earlier dream. "We lived a while, had
fun, raised families," Ryder says of her generation. "Now we
can go back and do what we really wanted to do—what our
parents argued against because it was too *impractical.*"

Beverly Ryder could be contemplating retirement after a
thirty-year management career in the private sector, looking
forward to traveling, dabbling in volunteer efforts, and getting some needed rest. But despite the temptation of a vacation, endless vacation isn't what she wants at this stage in her
life.

"Education is the civil rights movement of the twenty-
first century," she says resolutely. "We cannot afford as a
democracy to leave as many kids behind and unprepared as
we have."

Ryder remembers being in meetings in her past jobs,
standing up to argue for a particular action, while at the same
time thinking, *In the big picture, what is this really going to do?
How much will it really matter whether the decision is made one
way or another?* It was a refrain that became louder and more
insistent over time.

Ryder is clear: She enjoyed her earlier work, she liked her
colleagues and respected the two corporations where she
spent more than three decades, as well as the CEOs under
whom she served. They were good years. But the work didn't
matter as much as educating a generation of young people.

The Encore Pioneers

All across the country, a leading edge of baby boomers is breaking fresh ground in the search for purpose and contribution in the second half of life. Recognizing that adult lives now frequently outlast initial careers, they are taking this emerging reality and infusing it with new significance.

These women and men are organizing their lives in stark defiance of traditional expectations for the period beyond midlife work. Eschewing retirement in either traditional or reinvented forms, they are instead opting for work. But they are renegotiating this relationship in order to work in new ways, on new terms, and to new ends.

Win Craft spent his middle years managing an electronics company in Rhode Island. Then he hit the wall. "I felt like, 'OK, I sold 10,000 widgets today. What am I going to do tomorrow, sell 15,000 widgets?'" he told a reporter from the *Boston Globe*, adding, "That was no longer motivation. I was starting to feel very empty." He started asking new questions: "What can I do that has more meaning to the world, that has more humanity to it, where I can contribute something? In my head, I had this phrase: 'Chasing a dream, not a dollar.'" Craft ended up enrolling at Simmons College School of Social Work.

Prompted by such questions, Craft and others are assembling a new career phase that is unlikely to last as long as their earlier work but may in the end "weigh" just as much. It's a significant body of work, a career of ten, fifteen, or even twenty years that provides enough time to do something substantial. There's time to return to school for training, to have a misstep or two, to go through a necessary learning curve. And their commitment is long enough for employers to take a chance on bringing in someone from outside the field and giving him or her time to learn the ropes.

The people who recount their encore career journeys in this book come from a wide array of backgrounds. Sally Bingham went to college in her fifties and became an Episcopal priest to fuse her passions for pastoral and environmental work. Robert Chambers got fed up with being a used-car salesman and found a way to help low-income people buy reliable, fuel-efficient cars. Ed Speedling was a top hospital executive before he began working with homeless people on the streets of Philadelphia. Sandra Sessoms-Penny retired from the military to become a teacher. Leslie Hawke left a job at an Internet start-up company to go into the Peace Corps in Romania, which led her to start a project in that country helping women and children.

Some are taking existing skills and applying them to new ends, while others are launching entirely new vocations, or even creating new organizations and businesses as social entrepreneurs. Some are making the move from the private sector to the nonprofit world, while others are moving within the nonprofit sector, or from education to health care, or from the military to another form of public service, passing up retirement for another tour of duty.

Rejecting phased retirement, they are looking forward to

this next phase of work as a destination, not a way-station between the end of midlife work and the beginning of full-on retirement. Instead of phasing out they are focusing in, attempting to find more from work, not less: more flexibility, to be sure, but equally more meaning and greater impact.

Most aren't waiting to turn sixty-five before making this change. In fact, the 2005 MetLife Foundation/Civic Ventures New Face of Work survey of 1,000 Americans between fifty and seventy years old showed there is a widespread desire not only to make the move to more meaningful work focused on creating a better world but to do so between fifty and fifty-five, early enough so that individuals would have enough time to learn the ropes, have real impact, and develop a legacy.

These practical idealists are enjoying important benefits, and many are finding their footing without great upheaval. But baby boomers embarking on an encore career should not assume smooth sailing. Only 12 percent of adults in the New Face of Work study felt they would have an easy time finding work that used their skills to make a difference. Employers, generally, aren't helping. Up until now, almost all the dynamism, impetus, and drive has come from individuals themselves, as they refuse to put their lifetime of experience or their ideals prematurely out to pasture. Many still face a rocky road—characterized by poor pathways, ambivalent organizations, and often retrograde public policy.

To Beverly Ryder, being at the vanguard of a new impulse recalls her experience as part of the front line of women entering the corporate world in the early 1970s, when there wasn't much support and there were few women in senior positions to turn to for advice or guidance. "You simply had to feel your way along," she recalls.

That characterization applies equally to what Ryder is hearing from her peers today, as they forge ahead despite the barriers, looking for work that is significant and makes a difference. "For some reason our generation is saying, 'We've got to do something.' We can't just let it go," she says. "There is something that draws us in. The motivations are religious, social, political. Or as simple as 'I've just got to do it.'"

Start Making Sense

In his book *Working*, Studs Terkel observes that Americans get up and go to work each day every bit as much for "daily meaning" as for "daily bread."

By embodying a powerful dream about work in the second half of life, the encore career pioneers exemplify Terkel's point and they challenge us in a fundamental way: How might we develop a vision and realize a reality of work in the second half of life that makes a genuine virtue out of the growing necessity of extended working lives? A kind of engagement that lifts the spirit, inspiring individuals to work not just a year or two longer to help balance the financial scorecard, but ten, or fifteen, or twenty years longer—and not because they should do it or are being coerced to do so, but because they want to, because the work promises such deep significance, because Marge Piercy is right: Just as the pitcher "cries for water to carry," so many of us yearn for "work that is real."

Still, this emerging phenomenon is about more than personal fulfillment.

The individuals at the vanguard of the encore career trend represent a potential windfall of talent for a range of sectors in society desperate for human beings to do those things only human beings can do. Some are poised to bring new solutions to areas long plagued by outmoded approaches. Many others promise to be a much-needed workforce of human and social capital for fields experiencing crushing labor shortages, gaps already evident in areas like teaching and nursing—and projected to grow rapidly in nonprofit sector leadership and even government service.

What if this vast and growing cohort served not only to fill labor shortages but to invert the talent gap in these key areas, creating an abundance of human capital for those things that matter most? We're used to the fantasy of money being no object. What if time, talent, and experience were no object? That new equation might prompt entirely new approaches to solving seemingly intractable problems.

How many of America's nearly 76 million baby boomers will join this army for change, pursuing encore careers combining continued income and social impact? It's too soon to know, but even a very small percentage would be a very big number.

According to a survey conducted by AARP, more than half of those who intend to work after retirement said that "helping people" was a "very important" factor in their work plans. "Consulting," the stereotypical post-midlife job, was only half as popular as teaching, the top-ranked choice. Also ranking among the top ten most popular post-retirement occupations were nurse and child care worker.

When the New Face of Work study asked pre-boomers and leading-edge boomers what kind of work they wanted to do in their next phase of life, fully half said they were interested in taking jobs now or in the future to help improve the quality of life in their communities. Of those age fifty to fifty-nine, nearly 60 percent said they were interested in reordering their priorities to put social purpose and impact front and center. Indeed, for 20 percent, doing so was a top priority. Certainly, there's likely to be a gap between people's higher aspirations and their actual behavior, but a strong base of interest came through loud and clear.

If good intentions become reality, and millions of boomers pursue encore careers, they could, in effect, create a kind of tipping point for social change. Only 5 percent of the retiree population ever moved to retirement communities in the 1960s and 1970s, yet these individuals became the icons of a new lifestyle, the "Golden Years," one that resonated far beyond the walls of retirement communities.

But the protagonists of this book hold an even greater promise: They are revolutionaries in the redistribution of work—rebalancing responsibilities and contribution within individual lives and across age groups.

Demographer James Vaupel, director of the laboratory on longevity at Germany's Max Planck Institute, argues that just as "the twentieth century was a century of redistribution of income," the twenty-first "may be a century of redistribution of work." The encore pioneers, in demonstrating that the second half of adulthood can be a time of significant contribution—indeed for many the time when they do their most important work—prompt a radical question along the lines of Vaupel's point. Put another way: "Why not restructure our life cycles so that we take more leisure when we most need it, earlier on," asks Berkeley social scientist Ron Lee, "and less later on?"

Why is it that we load down individuals in their twenties, thirties, and forties with the expectation that they are most productive at precisely the juncture when we also ask them to raise children and climb up the income curve, while we essentially prod individuals from their fifties onward to stop working, or at the very least to please move out of the way?

Instead, why not refocus our public policies and other investments to better support young families and the frail elderly, while simultaneously expanding opportunities for those who want to continue contributing in significant ways? What we need is a fresh map of life, a new course that extends productivity much deeper into lives—while taking into full account the needs of those who are not able to continue working.

The encore career phenomenon and the individuals giving it shape suggest a redistribution of work not just within individual lives, but across age groups. Why should a shrinking group of adults in the middle generation take on the extraordinary weight of supporting or subsidizing everyone else? It's an equation that is already straining under an unbearable—and unfair—burden. By redistributing important, needed work to the encore generation while recapturing the vast investment in the human and social resources already made in this group, we create the prospect of a much larger population in the middle supporting children and the truly dependent elderly.

In short, by creating individual lives that make more sense, we can create a society that makes more sense.

The encore career trend holds the potential to dramatize such a shift in thinking and behavior, and to go one significant step further, providing a distinct and compelling answer to the question: "Why do we work?"

In part, to pay the bills and contribute to the economy. In part, also, to find a sense of direction, to connect with others, to enhance our identity. But equally, to have an impact—to work in ways that are not only personally meaningful but that mean something beyond oneself.

In choosing work that is aimed at making a better world, these leading-edge baby boomers are challenging the definition of success for all Americans. They stand to add weight and numbers to a gathering movement whose larger purpose is to solve the greatest problems facing humanity today.

As such, this impulse constitutes the boomers' last best hope to fulfill the promise of their generation, to answer the call to greatness, to leave the world a better place than they found it.

Velma Simpson

*Allstate Agent to U.S. Department of Housing
and Urban Development*

'd been a real estate insurance agent for Allstate for almost twenty years, working out of Longmont, Colorado. My husband, Steve, worked as an agent for ten years in the same office. We were doing well, making six figures. The thing is, I wasn't a typical insurance agent. My manager, my clients, and my staff used to joke that I was really a social worker who just happened to sell insurance. And that was reflected in my clientele. I did have some corporate and commercial clients, but the majority of my clients were average folks, a lot of low-income folks, a lot of seniors, and a lot of immigrants. I enjoyed my work. I enjoyed the people. I enjoyed advocating for them and helping them try to solve problems. I enjoyed beating my head against the wall with Allstate, trying to get them to change some of their ways of doing things, recognizing that building relationships with your clients was why people stayed.

I initially got into the insurance business after Steve was diagnosed with melanoma. At that time I was a stay-at-home mom with three children; our youngest was not quite two. And I suddenly realized that Steve might not always be there. In 1981 I set about trying to find a job to support my family if it came to that. I was thirty-three with three kids, and I found it very difficult to find one. I had graduated [from Colorado State University] cum laude. I had been very active in my community. Yet I found it difficult to find work after staying at home with my young children. I finally did get a job, working for a small community as an administrative assistant. I left at 5:30 in the morning, and the kids had to manage to get themselves to the school bus, because Steve was a truck driver at that time. But I just wasn't making any money. I got into insurance because I had to find something that could truly replace his income if I became the sole breadwinner.

When I was fifty-two and Steve was fifty-one, we took another look at our lives. I asked him what he'd really like to be doing, and he said teaching theater in college. So I said, "Why aren't we doing it?" And we set about getting him in school.

Steve left Longmont to pursue a master's degree in theater at the University of Oklahoma in Norman. Initially, the idea was that we'd live apart while he got his degree. The first year, he went to Oklahoma, and I stayed in Colorado and continued to run the insurance business. Then the opportunity to sell the business presented itself after he had been down there for a year, and I took it. Part of what made me start to be less happy at my job was that everything was becoming computerized, and my advocacy was no longer valued. I couldn't talk to the underwriter. I couldn't talk to the claims people and say we shouldn't cancel this policy, or explain why this claim should be paid and here's why.

Everything had been put into a matrix in the computer, and whatever the computer said went. So that forced me to become almost a high-paid data entry operator. The only focus of the company was the bottom line, and that wasn't why I was there. So it ceased to be fulfilling to me. I was no longer so focused on the money. If that was really all I was getting out of the deal, it wasn't enough.

I initially went to Oklahoma to join Steve, having no real clue what I was going to do. Except I thought, with my entrepreneurial background and experience as a community activist, I could probably become an executive director someplace. But, it turned out I needed a master's degree.

I was interested in working in a social services position, maybe with a women's shelter. I had volunteered on a crisis line for domestic violence. I had served on a board of directors of a homeless transitional housing organization. I thought about jobs that dealt with domestic violence and homelessness.

So I went back to school. I found a program at the University of Oklahoma that I could complete about the same time as Steve's program. We both got our master's degrees, and then Steve started looking for a doctoral program. He was fortunate enough to be admitted to Florida State, one of the best theater schools in the nation.

When he was admitted, I applied for a number of jobs down in Florida, but none came through. Then serendipity came into play. I happened to see an e-mail sent to Steve about the Presidential Management Fellows program in the federal government. I saw it over his shoulder, and it caught my attention. He was going through and deleting mail. But I happened to see it and said, "Wait! That sounds interesting to me."

The dean of my master's program nominated me and I was offered a position working on homelessness at HUD [Department of Housing and Urban Development]. It was a perfect fit. They asked me, "Why do you want to do this?" And I understood in my soul it was something I had been carrying since the 1960s. I demonstrated against the war. I worked for Eugene McCarthy and George McGovern, and I had incorporated into my life the words of John Kennedy. I told them I was responding to the call I had heard all those years ago, to ask not what your country can do for you, but what you can do for your country.

It just felt like what I was supposed to be doing. Steve and I have both had doors open when it was time for the door to be there. Whether that's God, whether that's the universe, whether that's serendipity, whether it's a fluke, I don't know. I don't know how these things happened.

I moved to Washington, D.C., to work for HUD, Steve was still in school at Florida State, and I rented a room from a woman and her teenage daughter. I was depleting our savings quickly, so I took a second job where I lived with an elderly woman and cared for her. I would leave HUD after work, go to her home and care for her overnight and full-time on the weekends. I did that for a year.

Living apart from Steve was harder than I had ever imagined. We had been together since high school. I was nearly alone for the first time in my life. I'm the oldest of eight kids; isolation and solitude were never part of my life. Even though I was sharing space with people, some of the silence I kind of liked. Steve and I both developed separate ways of doing things for the first time in our lives. After that year, Steve was able to move to Washington, and we stayed there until he was diagnosed with prostate cancer. We've been in treatment since and he's currently in remission.

Through all of this, I've learned to trust my instincts. I remember always wondering how do you know when you are called? Does God appear? I didn't understand. I've seen things fall into place, but it's so difficult to trust or have confidence that they will. I remember speaking to a spiritual counselor. I told her, "I feel like I'm standing at the edge of a chasm." And she said, "Spread your wings and fly." And I have tried to keep that in my mind. To have the courage to step into that chasm.

Selling our business and selling our house were big decisions, and a lot of our friends thought we were crazy. That counselor's words have continued to buoy me at times when I'm not sure. When Steve was diagnosed with cancer, I really wasn't sure. We're back at a chasm, but we're continuing to fly.

CHAPTER TWO

Inventing
the Golden Years

Walter Reuther, the legendary labor leader, was on the offensive when he took the podium in Milwaukee to address his autoworker union brothers and sisters in July 1949. Four years after the end of World War II, the national economy was volatile, with rising unemployment paired with rampant inflation. Still unionized workers hoped to make major postwar gains. Just before the convention, the United Steelworkers of America had won a major strike, gaining the right to negotiate pension benefits for the first time. Now telegrams were arriving from autoworker locals, reporting overwhelming votes in favor of a strike against Ford Motor Company.

The planned action against Ford was to be a test of Reuther's strategy for winning the same new benefit for autoworkers—a guaranteed pension. The union was demanding $100 a month, on top of Social Security, Reuther said, so a worker would "be able to retire with a semblance of security and human dignity in his old age."

Reuther warmed up by taking aim not at Ford, but at C. E. "Engine Charlie" Wilson, the president of General Motors, best remembered for his often misquoted line, "What's good for the country is good for General Motors, and vice versa." Reuther reported Wilson's 1948 salary, including bonuses: $516,000, the equivalent of $258 an hour. On top of that, GM had promised Wilson a pension of $25,000 a year.

With deadpan delivery, Reuther told the story of a bull on Wilson's farm. The bull had a bad back. "We are sorry about that," Reuther said, and he explained how GM had arranged for a 140,000-volt X-ray machine to be flown to Detroit and driven to the farm, only to find there wasn't enough electricity to hook it up and diagnose the bull's problem. So Detroit Edison ran a special power line.

Why wasn't such care available to everybody, Reuther asked. "It is because C. E. Wilson's bull cost $16,000, and you get boys and workers for free."

Reuther continued, "They say to the worker when he is too old to work and too young to die, 'You cannot have security in your old age. If you make $258 an hour, they give it to you; if you make $1.65 an hour they say, 'You don't need it, you are not entitled to it, and we are not going to give it to you.'"

Reuther vowed, "We are going to change that in America, and we are going to start in the next couple of weeks."

And he did. By September 1949, the UAW had won a $100-a-month pension from Ford for those with thirty years of service. Reuther's phrase "too old to work and too young to die" had become the somewhat ironic rallying cry for the broad movement to secure workers' retirement.

The spread of the corporate pension helped seal an implicit social contract. Decades of wrangling—from the trauma of the Great Depression, through the bitter auto, steel, and miners' strikes of the postwar era to the creation of Medicare in 1965 and beyond—resulted in a deal. Corporations and unions, conservatives and liberals, younger people and older adults themselves came to expect that loyal employees and responsible citizens could anticipate a comfortable retirement free of worry about slipping into poverty because of old age or ill health.

Later, cracks and then chasms opened up in that retirement framework. But for decades, the system, fractured and uneven as it was, worked well. Over time, the infusion of resources into a population that had forever been resource starved helped to underwrite a social transformation of historic proportions.

For the first time, workers would have guaranteed income in their later years. Social Security would provide a financial safety net for most (though certainly not all) Americans. Prudent planners put money into savings accounts as well. And for the many workers spending their entire careers with a single employer, a corporate pension provided additional cushion.

As the nation's older population was transformed over the 1950s and 1960s into a bastion of the leisured life, whole industries were transformed, from television to travel. A new political constituency was born, and social policy adapted. The nature of work, even the goal of work itself, was changed in the process.

Retirement became the great national repository of deferred gratification, the fun-filled payoff for all those years of hard work. It was the liberation from labor, graying as playing. Indeed, retirement got more and more comfortable as the ascendancy of the postwar U.S. economy allowed more generous pension payments, both from the government and employers, and as employers became even more eager to get older workers out of the labor force. Paying them to leave helped make way for a baby boom of younger, lower-paid employees.

The combination of financial incentives and cultural norms changed how Americans lived. In 1950, nearly half the men over sixty-five remained in the workforce. By 2000, less than 18 percent were still working. Retirement had become a bedrock American institution, and individuals scrambled to get to that promised land as quickly as possible.

The Roleless Role

Today, we have to remember that the dream of retirement as an endless vacation did not always exist, that later years were dreaded as a sure slide into poverty or as time spent idly on the margins of society, bereft of any sense of purpose or role in life. For much of American history, for most Americans, there had been no such thing as retirement. Most individuals worked until they dropped.

That was the case in the Puritan colonies, a subsistence agrarian economy that was dependent on using all the able-bodied individuals available. However, the Puritans went further. They didn't simply view their older population as extra pairs of hands in a society that didn't have a single person to waste. They revered these older citizens as paragons of wisdom.

The Puritans thought that a "hoary head is a crown of gold." A ripe old age was a sign from the divine, an indication that one had lived a life of grace and was closer to God. The Puritans went to great lengths to express this reverence. They depicted Jesus in flowing white locks; they wore white wigs and cut their clothes so the shoulders slumped, even lying on the census to say they were three or four years older than they were (we do the opposite today). Historians of early American life describe a "gerontocracy" in which older people held on to power and productive roles based not only on a legal system but on a culture that upheld the benefits of age and experience.

The nineteenth century saw an end to this order, and by the early twentieth century, through cultural upheaval and expert opinion, older people began to be viewed as hopeless, pathetic figures with little to offer. Historian W. Andrew Achenbaum quotes an economist who wrote in 1906 that the older worker was "slow, hesitating, frequently half-blind and deaf . . . sadly misplaced amidst the death-dealing machinery of a modern factory." What's more, the factories based wages on a seniority system, and given assembly-line production, older workers were paid far more for the same tasks as younger workers standing beside them on the line. Mandatory retirement was introduced as a counterbalance.

This combination of forces pushed many older workers out of the labor force and into a far from secure retirement. For the vast majority of these people, retirement did not mean leisure. It meant desperate poverty. Never particularly secure, nearly one-fourth of older Americans were living in poverty in 1910. In the depths of the Depression, one-half of all older people were in poverty and the number grew to two-thirds by 1940, when the first Social Security checks were distributed. Many older adults were driven to live with their children, forcing young families to accommodate another generation, often in cramped quarters. The poorhouse had become a real prospect for many Americans in their sixties and seventies.

The Great Depression revealed just how fragile the safety net in this country was for older people. But they weren't alone. Youth unemployment skyrocketed, feeding fears of significant social disruption, even revolution, in the absence of gainful employment for restless and destitute young men. Even before he was elected, Franklin D. Roosevelt stressed that a new social contract, a "new deal," was needed.

"Faith in America, faith in our tradition of personal responsibility, faith in our institutions, faith in ourselves demands that we recognize the new terms of the old social contract," Roosevelt declared in his 1932 speech to the Commonwealth Club in San Francisco. "We must do so, lest a rising tide of misery engendered by our common failure engulf us all. But failure is not an American habit; and in the strength of great hope we must all shoulder our common load."

In a burst of energy in his first hundred days, Roosevelt pushed through legislation to create the Civilian Conservation Corps, the Works Progress Administration (WPA), and other New Deal programs to put the country to work. But Roosevelt continued to receive thousands of letters from the elderly poor, many of them requesting a loan, not a gift.

"I have worked hard all my life, and bad luck has overtaken me in my old days, and I wanted to see if you could help me get a little relief, so I can get me a team and make a crop this next year," one seventy-two-year-old man beseeched the president. "You know that I need it or I would not ask for it."

By 1935, Roosevelt was ready to propose Social Security. His Committee on Economic Security, five cabinet officers led by Labor Secretary Frances Perkins, found, "For those now old, insecurity is doubly tragic, because they are beyond the productive period. . . . With a rapidly increasing number and percentage of the aged, and the impairment and loss of savings, this country faces, in the next decades, an even greater old-age security problem than that with which it is already confronted."

The notion of greater security for older adults had support from many quarters. Encouraging older people to leave the labor market would open positions for young people, reducing the number of idle hands and providing lower-wage workers for businesses—and new members for unions. Social Security was a measured response to even more radical proposals, such as Francis E. Townsend's "Townsend Clubs," which demanded that the government provide $200 a month for every citizen over sixty, and Senator Huey Long's proposed "Share our Wealth" plan, which included pensions for the elderly along with $2,000 a year for every family. The fact that Long had signed up 7 million followers by 1935 indicates the strength of the ferment.

Roosevelt rallied Americans to fight the Depression the same way he later rallied them to fight World War II, by appealing to them to look beyond their own self-interest to a greater common purpose. As Jonathan Alter shows in *The Defining Moment*, Roosevelt used his confidence "to win power, restore hope, and redefine the bargain—the 'Deal'— the country struck with its own people. The result was a new notion of social obligation, especially in a crisis." Social Security was part of a "new social contract" that FDR felt was necessary to save American democracy. Risk, rather than being borne solely by individuals, was to be borne by society as a whole. Social Security was intended to protect those who were frail, dependent, and unable to work, not to set up a significant segment of the population as a permanent leisure class.

The New Deal, Michael Tomasky writes in the *American Prospect*, "was a period when citizens were asked to contribute to a project larger than their own well-being. And, crucially, it was a period when citizens (a majority of them, at least) reciprocally understood themselves to have a stake in this larger project." The model was not to hand out benefits and turn citizens into dependent wards. Rather, "Social Security and all the jobs programs and rural electrification plans and federal mortgage-insurance programs were examples of the state giving people the tools to improve their own lives while improving the collective life of the country," Tomasky writes.

Still, union leaders such as Walter Reuther knew they were on dangerous ground, even as they laid the foundation for the new retirement system. Reuther accepted company-supported pensions only as a fallback from his much-preferred approach, which would have shared the risk among many employers, either regionally or nationally. Reuther hoped that the demographic time bomb that was certain to send corporate pension costs skyrocketing would eventually bring employers around.

A Season in Search of a Purpose

By the time World War II ended, the years between the end of work and the end of life were beginning to stretch for many Americans. The idea of setting sixty-five as the age for receiving Social Security borrowed from Otto von Bismarck, who had set that age for eligibility for the Prussian Military Pension he established in the 1870s. Given life expectancies of that era, Bismarck was convinced that the state would never have to pay for a single pension.

In 1940, the first Social Security check was issued to Ida M. Fuller, a retired bookkeeper living in Ludlow, Vermont, who had contributed all of $24.75 into the system. By the time she died, at age 100, she had drawn $22,888.92 in benefits, according to historian Achenbaum. So much for the actuarial tables.

But for those who were "too old to work and too young to die," the growing years after retirement were becoming a wasteland, an extended, empty anteroom between the end of work and the end of life. Experts advised older Americans to lead a quiet life, stay out of the way, and perhaps rock on their porches like Whistler's Mother. Ernest Burgess of the University of Chicago, the preeminent academic commentator on retirement in the 1940s and 1950s, described the period of loose ends as a "roleless role." Individuals had greater health, longevity, and economic security but suffered from a lack of purpose.

Lewis Mumford, the great social critic, lamented that for

the longer-living Americans, "The years that have been added to their portion have come, unfortunately, at the wrong end of their lives." In May 1956, Mumford wrote, "Probably at no period and in no culture have the old ever been so completely rejected as in our own country, during the last generation." As life was extended, misery was extended with it, Mumford said. "Unwanted in the cramped small home, even when they are loved, and too often unloved because they are unwanted, the aged find their lives progressively meaningless and empty, while their days ironically lengthen."

In a prescient prescription, Mumford fifty years ago advocated "giving them opportunities to form new social ties," as well as "functions and duties that draw on their precious life experience and put it to new uses." He quoted Tennyson's "Ulysses": "Old age hath yet his honor and his toil."

By the early 1960s, the increases in both longevity and economic security had combined to create a new mass social institution, retirement, but not yet the new meanings to fill it. A cover story in *Time* magazine written from Fair Haven, New Jersey, described a retiree, "not what anybody would call an old man. His hair is gray, but not white, his face is lined, not wrinkled. He sits on his son's porch, while his granddaughter is absorbed in play. He looks down at 'strong, freckled' hands and wonders: 'I don't know what to do with myself these days.'"

Bewildered, he continues, "I'm supposed to be old—I was 65 last fall—but God knows I don't feel old. The company is right about the retirement age, I suppose; it has to make places for younger men. But what happens to us?"

The everyman retiree could have been anywhere in the United States. "His cry and his question are being heard more often and urgently everywhere—in Southern drawl and Northern twang, in city and suburb, cold-water flat and executive suite," *Time* wrote. A former factory foreman explained dejectedly: "I can't think of anything useful I can do anymore, and I don't want to sit around doing nothing. So I just sleep for longer spells, hoping it will end."

Another man, relocated to the gray haven of St. Petersburg, Florida, offered his personal prescription for coping with later life. "What you do is sleep good and late in the morning. That way I eat breakfast for lunch about 11 o'clock, and then I don't have to eat lunch at all. Sure I'm lonely. But it's better to be lonely here in all this sunshine than back in Cincinnati."

It fell to the wizards of financial services and consumer marketing to define a compelling vision for retirement, one that went beyond economic security and extended lifespans to the question the pioneering gerontologist Robert Butler would ask two decades later: "Why survive?"

This was a question that had become increasingly urgent for millions of Americans entering their fifties and sixties by mid-century, consigned to protracted uselessness and loath to think about the grim era between work and death. And pressure was building as the numbers of these individuals grew larger and the period of roleless roles more protracted. It was an awkward time for them and for their families.

It was just as uncomfortable for the pension business.

Financial services companies were having trouble selling retirement products to individuals reluctant to contemplate the dreaded state, much less invest in it. In response, the industry put on a concerted effort to transform the meaning of retirement, to do something extraordinarily bold: actually convince people that it was something to look forward to. It was the first American effort to reinvent retirement.

As early as 1952, H. G. Kenagy, vice president of Mutual Life Insurance Co., in a speech to the National Industrial Conference Board, applauded corporate newsletters and magazines for employees for doing "a splendid job selling the idea . . . that old age can be beautiful, and that the best of life is yet to come." Most effective, he said, were "constant stories of happily retired people telling what they do, but still more, of course, emphasizing what they did to get ready for the life they are now living." His pitch: America's major corporations should begin preparing employees for retirement at age fifty.

In particular, marketers seized on the notion of aristocratic leisure, depicting retirement not as a fate for people too old to work but as an age of liberation—from responsibility, from work, from the constraints of midlife. It was the chance for a second childhood, the endless vacation.

In 1951, the Corning Corporation convened a group of scholars to help make sense of the relationship between retirement and leisure. The session chairman, Mills College president Lynn White Jr., concluded by urging a major effort designed "to glamorize leisure as we have not." In the campaigns that followed, those approaching retirement were subjected to a "barrage of propaganda" about the wonders of this new life phase. For example, men were tantalized with the prospect of being able to go to the ball game not only in the middle of the week, but in the middle of the afternoon.

The financial services companies' extensive marketing efforts succeeded in elevating the idea that retirement was not something to be feared or dreaded, but rather the opposite: a new version of the American Dream. Older people weren't the detritus of society, too old to work yet too young to die. Rather, they were the first American mass aristocrats. The pitch, says historian William Graebner, was quite a pivot: Retirement need not be a sign of incompetence or maladjustment but rather "a bounty bestowed by the society and by the pension."

Inventing the Golden Years

Through the 1950s, the financial services industry helped to set the stage for change in the essence of retirement, but the transformation in attitudes and behavior they aspired to remained a few years off. In this case, it is actually possible, amid the swirl of broader trends, shifting economic conditions, and expansion of programs like Social Security, to isolate the turning point—the place, and the date, even the person most responsible.

On January 1, 1960, a developer named Delbert E. Webb

opened the world's first large-scale retirement community, Sun City, in what was a cotton field outside of Peoria, Arizona. Webb was an extraordinary figure. The son of a carpenter from Fresno, California, he grew up obsessed with baseball and determined to become a professional ballplayer. A hulking figure at six foot five, a man with relentless drive, he worked as a carpenter himself for construction companies that sponsored semi-pro baseball teams. It was a way to support his obsession. He had the size, the willpower, and the opportunity to make it in baseball. Unfortunately, he had little talent for the game. He might have gone on for years longer on resolve alone, but he was hit with typhoid fever in his late twenties while working in the shipyards of Oakland, California, and was sent to Phoenix to recuperate—or to die.

It spelled the end of Webb's baseball-playing days—he shrank during his illness from well over 200 pounds to close to ninety—and launched the career of one of America's great entrepreneurs. Two years after being dispatched to Phoenix with poor prospects of survival, Webb's newly created construction company was building the annex to the Arizona state capital. In the upcoming years he would go on to build Madison Square Garden, the Houston Space Complex, the Beverly Hilton, and many of the Japanese internment camps (his response to criticism: "A job's a job."). He invented the motel, owned the New York Yankees during their most successful period of 1946 through 1964 (ten world championships spanning the era of DiMaggio and Mantle), and built Las Vegas (in the film *Bugsy*, it is "Del Webb's Flamingo" that Bugsy Siegel is developing—it's said that Siegel assuaged Webb's worries about Siegel's mob ties by explaining, "We only kill each other.").

Webb, more than any other figure, invented retirement as we know it, bringing together a pair of skills that he may well have inherited from his two grandfathers—one of whom was a leading English evangelist of his day, the key figure in building California's first irrigation system. Webb combined marketing genius and stunning entrepreneurship with a keen appreciation of the historical moment. And when it came to the transformation of retirement, he was at the top of his game. His company, coupling marketing prowess with the ability to build housing communities on a vast scale, invented the defining phrase of the era, "the Golden Years."

Webb had an intuitive understanding that things were about to break and that the discontent of a large and growing group of retirees on the margins of society, with little idea what to do with themselves and living longer than ever, constituted an entrepreneurial opportunity. He did little research on the trend, simply dispatching one of his lieutenants to talk to discontented retirees inhabiting the park benches of St. Petersburg, Florida, before sinking $2 million (in late-1950s dollars) into creating a seniors-only enclave in the godforsaken area on the outskirts of dusty, scorching Phoenix.

Webb's approach was to build modest tract houses surrounded by a golf course and make them affordable to working- and middle-class Americans, ranging from Walter

Reuther's retired UAW members and their peers to middle-class professionals from the East Coast and Midwest. The effort was geared toward providing them with a sense of community, better weather, and most of all, as their marketing efforts trumpeted: "An Active New Way of Life." The complexes offered not only golf, but shuffleboard, bowling, and swimming pools. Webb summoned the nation's retirees off their porches and gave them something else in the process, the chance to forget their age. If everyone was "old"—or as Webb told them "55 and Better!"—then no one was old, and age ceased to matter as a differentiating characteristic.

Still, despite millions of dollars and years of building and preparation, Webb and his team were feeling increasingly uneasy as Sun City's January 1, 1960, opening drew closer. They remembered that every gerontologist and psychiatrist they consulted had told them that their idea was a bad one, that it would never fly. The nation's oldsters would never abandon their homes and families to move halfway across the country to live in an age-segregated enclave.

These concerns came crashing home the night before Sun City was set to open, on New Year's Eve 1959, as a group of Webb Company top executives sat silently around a dinner table at Manuel's Place, a Mexican restaurant in Peoria, outside Phoenix. Breaking the uncomfortable silence around the table at Manuel's, Owen Childress, the manager responsible for sales at Sun City, finally gave voice to a central worry that had been plaguing him for months: "How am I going to get a 30-year mortgage on a guy who is 65 years old?"

The next morning, the group showed up to view a scene they could never have imagined. Lined up, for miles on end, were cars filled with older men and women, converging on Sun City from all over the country. As the line stretched, the cars waited to enter the converted cotton field where five model homes, tiny Levittown-style houses christened The Nottingham and The Monticello, sat awkwardly on the edge of a makeshift golf course.

By the end of the weekend, 100,000 people in all turned up.

·　　　·　　　·

From those small blades of putting-green grass and that collection of modest homes would spring an entire industry built around the Golden Years dream of retirement as leisure. Scarcely more than a decade had passed since the autoworkers and steelworkers had secured the first union pensions, and a retirement of leisure had become the new American Dream. By August 1962, when *Time* magazine again took up the subject of the aging of America, its cover declared: "The Retirement City: A New Way of Life for the Old." Del Webb's face shone against a backdrop of shuffleboard courts and palm fronds, all symbols of new active-retirement living.

Time's readers were introduced to Sun City residents like Dr. Chester L. Meade, "a tanned, lithe" man who gave up his dental practice in Mason City, Iowa, to move to Sun City with his wife, Mabel. The Meades said they missed some of their friends from Iowa, but now they were able to build their lives around recreation. "Back there," the retired dentist explained, "you can play golf only a few months of the year. The rest of the time you go to the Elks Club and play two-bit rummy."

In this environment, idleness no longer stood in contrast to productivity. Another Sun City denizen, Dean Babbitt, formerly of New Hampshire, added that he and his neighbors were on the front end of a new vision of retirement: "People here have pulled up stakes and started over. Whether you're living on Social Security or a bunch of money, it makes no difference."

Soon the Golden Years lifestyle—spurred by continued prosperity, the expansion of private pensions and Social Security, and the advent of Medicare—began to radiate throughout the country. In some states, such as Arizona, half the residents over fifty-five lived in age-segregated communities like Sun City and Leisure World. But nationally only 5 to 10 percent of the older population ever chose to relocate to the Sunbelt or to retirement communities. Very few were willing to separate from their extended families or familiar surroundings, to move to the seventh green of a golf-course community catering to retirees. Still, those individuals living the pure, distilled essence of the leisure life became aspirational models for millions of others, who might not move onto the golf course but began building their lives around leisure nonetheless.

Once communities like Webb's Sun City and its chief rival, Leisure World, emerged as emblems of retirement, a vast leisure sector followed. In a relatively brief period, these interests transformed the ideal of retirement into one of endless vacation. They managed to turn a dreaded period into something to look forward to, to transform a push into a pull, to make a virtue out of a necessity.

And a remarkable transformation it was, as the goal of retirement was soon supplanted by a new dream: early retirement. Millions dropped out of the labor market as soon as they could, until the numbers of men over sixty-five in the workforce dropped below 20 percent. At the same time, retirees emerged as the biggest consumers of leisure activities in America. Studies by John Robinson at Penn State and William Godby at the University of Maryland found that half the free time liberated by retirement went into watching television, with gardening in second place.

The older population had become the nation's true leisure class.

Too Much of a Good Thing?

When the writer Calvin Trillin visited Sun City a few years after it opened, he was struck by the frantic "busyness" of its residents—rushing around from one activity to the next as if to block out an emptiness in their lives. Indeed, Trillin challenged one of Webb's executives, Tom Breen, on the seeming obsession of Sun City residents with activity, almost any activity: "I asked Breen if he had considered the possibility that he had created a community dedicated to self-indulgence on an unprecedented scale, a place in which the distinction in value among various kinds of activities had all but disappeared."

Indeed, the frantic busyness of retirement community residents was being reproduced in the outside world of retirees. Sociologist David Ekerdt of the University of Kansas calls this phenomenon "the busy ethic," a way for retirees imbued with the work ethic yet without any real role in life to maintain a sense of continuity with their previous lives. According to Ekerdt, "Marketers, with the golf club as their chief prop, have been instrumental in fostering the busy image," adding that "one cannot talk to retirees for very long without hearing the rhetoric of busyness."

In defense of retirement communities like Sun City and Leisure World, and the broader activity ethic that followed in their wake, the "active new way of life" was a dramatic step forward from the passive old way that preceded it. We now know that activity, recreation, and exercise are key ingredients in living healthier, happier, and longer lives. Considering that this point is still being rediscovered in headlines about a new generation of older people being more active, promoting physical fitness and leisure sports a half century ago was an enormous breakthrough.

The problem was that the new focus on activity was not

able to close the gulf in meaning and roles between the end of work and the end of life, to fill the void produced by the absence of work. Opportunities around lifelong learning and volunteering that developed through the 1960s and 1970s served to partially alleviate the "purpose gap." Still, they offered only partial solutions. All too often, senior volunteer programs were aimed at "keeping the old folks busy," providing another form of leisure and activity without significant impact beyond keeping individuals from getting bored.

As life and health have become further extended over the final decades of the twentieth century and into the twenty-first, the old lifestyle is no longer sustainable. The Golden Years concept was never designed to support a period as long as midlife in duration; it was supposed to be a pleasant way for individuals who had worked in much more physically demanding jobs than today's fifty- and sixty-somethings to get a well-deserved rest before disability set in. Three decades of the "busy ethic" is a fate that many today would deeply prefer to avoid—and that very few can afford.

The Golden Years was also ill-suited for a population explosion of aging boomers. Today, many analysts conclude that if huge numbers of baby boomers adopt the Golden Years retirement ethic, we'll be on the road to social collapse.

If graying continues to mean only playing, it will mean paying, as many today claim. Those wringing their hands about the coming "demographic overload" are right, in part: We can't afford a leisure class that makes up one-fourth of the population. Indeed, if social arrangements and cultural ideals designed to drive workers out of the labor force remain in force in the upcoming decades, the gloomiest of the predictions is likely to come true.

But there's hope. A new set of structural forces is emerging—as profound as the ones that gave birth to the postwar ideal of the "Golden Years." Like the first retirees to flock to Sun City, the pioneers of the new model are finding their way through largely uncharted territory. But unlike those retirees, these pioneers are not celebrating their freedom *from* work, but rather their freedom *to* work, in ways that hold the promise of personal fulfillment, economic benefit, and social renewal.

Robert Chambers

*Car Salesman
to Social Entrepreneur*

was on the USS *Kitty Hawk* during the Vietnam War. When you're running very heavy operations, an aircraft carrier is a very dangerous place to be. At times I had to work seventy-two hours without sleeping to keep these planes working. The pilot's life depended on me fixing that airplane. I was an electronics technician. I was working really hard, but I was also an adventurous sort. I saved up leave and every time we'd pull into base I would take vacation.

In the Philippines, I saw poverty like I had never seen before. I came to understood what poverty meant, and it just left an indelible brand. At that time most middle-class Americans had no concept of what real poverty was. Today we can see some of what's happening in Africa on television, but at the time there wasn't coverage. We could read it in the papers and we could see some pictures, but really seeing kids begging, not having enough to eat. How skinny they were, how unhealthy they looked just left a deep impression on me.

We were in a big naval base in the southern Philippines. There was a place where you were allowed to go as sailors when you were off ship temporarily. We could go into town and have a drink or two. One night the shore patrol came and said everybody had to walk home because there was a strike of the taxi jitneys. So you had to walk and leave a little early to make sure you got back to the ship on time.

The jitney strike was going on in the central square. And there were a couple jitneys that were breaking the strike, and there were some sailors on the back of this one jitney, and as I'm walking through this square, I see one of the men pull the driver out of that vehicle, put a gun against his head and blow his brains out. I wasn't five feet away from him when that happened. It terrified me to see that sort of violence and passion in dealing with something like a strike.

I went to college at Auburn University in Alabama. I worked two jobs and had federal support when I went to school full-time. [But] financial pressure forced me to quit school and move back to Atlanta before my senior year. I was in a five-year engineering program and always thought about going back to finish, but it just never happened.

When I left Auburn, I went to work maintaining electrical circuits for AT&T for a very brief period. You've never seen a more regimented place in your life. I was given an assignment to wire some circuits and do some testing. It was a three-month assignment and I got all my work done in about two weeks. I went back to my supervisor, asking what should I work on next. She said, "Look busy."

Well, I wasn't the sort who tried to look busy. I went to work for a bank and a friend of mine who had just started a computer time-sharing business. Next I helped put the first computer line across the U.S.-Canadian border. Later I worked for a subsidiary at Dartmouth, in Hanover, New Hampshire, also in the computer business, and then set up a software company in New York to service banks. That got into some financial difficulties. Do you remember Black Monday? Within a week of Black Monday all the purchasing agents called and said, "We're not buying anything ever again or until things change."

I moved back to Hanover because I owned a condo there. I was burned out on the computer industry at that point, even though I was a knowledgeable executive. I really liked the environment in New Hampshire. I had some resources, but I'm not wealthy. I could have retired but it would have been really tight, besides I'm not the type to do that. I had this friend I'd met through a bike-riding group who was working in the car business. He said why don't you come into the car business? You work well with people and we need someone over here with your computer background. Maybe you can help us with e-commerce. *All right,* I thought, *I'll give it a try.*

I sold cars for five years, beginning in the mid-nineties. It's a brutal business. There are questionable practices even in the best dealerships. There are some really good people in the car business, but selling cars is on the shadier side of real business.

I was disillusioned even very early by the way I saw some people being treated. They also expect you to work seven days a week, and being away from my family every weekend was something I didn't like doing. I was initially disillusioned with the industry because of the pressure to work Saturdays and Sundays, but the disillusionment really took hold over the treatment of poor people.

I'm sitting in these sales meetings. If the management wants to sell a particular vehicle they'll put a $1,000 bonus on that car. Every salesman is trying to sell that car. Is that the right car for a particular customer? It doesn't matter because the business has refined their sales techniques over a hundred years to get you into a car, to get you to like it, and to get you to sign the paper and drive out of there in one day.

Poor people really don't get a fair shake when they come in to a dealership. Every car salesman in the business is commissioned. Dealers make more money from used cars than they do from new cars. A high-end buyer doesn't even want to look at the used cars. But the salesman takes a poor person over to the oldest, most decrepit vehicle because that's often the most profitable one. The dealer has taken it as a trade-in for maybe $1,000 and they're reselling it for $5,000. They've put about

$400 or $500 into fixing the brakes and muffler. And maybe it's got 80,000 or 90,000 miles on it. It's in poor shape. That low-income person is never introduced to the new car.

I tried to direct people to new vehicles. I learned that the banks offer interest rates so a new-car purchaser pays a lower interest rate than someone who buys a slightly used car and they tier it so that a six-year-old car with 90,000 miles comes with a very high interest rate. And they tier interest on your credit score. You go back fifteen years ago and everybody paid the same interest. But as the banks got more information from computers, they segmented more. They do risk-based lending.

My friend Leo and I ride bikes together in the morning, and we started talking about this. He worked in the industry and he was disillusioned as well. We started talking about how we could set up a business that would help poor people buy cars. We debated whether we could we get enough clients to make something like this work. Could we raise enough money to get started? We talked for a year. We even started talking to some banks. I came up with an idea about guaranteeing the loans. And we knew that focusing on new, fuel-efficient cars was where we wanted to go because there was really longer-lasting value there than anywhere else in this deal. We also knew if we could get them the new car at a reasonable interest rate, then it would have a tremendous payoff: They're going to save a lot of money. But we wondered, how do we get banks to agree to do this?

A turning point came when the family that owned the dealership—they were good people and didn't really bless the shady things going on—decided to sell it. They had inherited it.

A guy came in to the dealership whom the sales people called a "woodchuck," which is what they'd call people from the country. They took him over to these old cars. And this was a guy who was not super-intelligent, but a hard worker. He was living in the backwoods where you need a vehicle to get around and he was sold this old car. The salesman made a big commission. It was one of those where they were paying a bonus commission if you sell this particular car. They made $3,500 on the vehicle itself.

Then the guy went into the business office and the manager offered him a loan with a high interest rate. I watched this and it just made me sick. They sell products, extended warranties, at really high profit margins and insurance that you might pay a thousand bucks for, but that an insurance agent can get for fifty, that sort of thing.

The business manager really rolled this guy and made a couple of thousand dollars off of him. The business manager and the salesman came out and they high-fived. I watched this guy driving off in a car that was going to die within a year—and he signed a loan for five years. How can you do this to people? I quit within a week.

It's a systemic failure, especially when you think of repairs and fuel economy. I'm an engineer. I like to analyze these things. That low-income individual is more often in a job where he doesn't get paid if he doesn't show up for work. When his car fails, not only does he have expenses for repairs, he doesn't get paid and he's getting a bad reputation for not showing up at work. So where's the fairness in that?

That really was the impetus for starting Bonnie CLAC, the nonprofit we created to provide low-interest loans and fuel-efficient cars to the rural poor living in New Hampshire.

Leo and I got the door slammed in our faces over and over again, but my tolerance for risk is probably higher than many people's. (My wife is the opposite, but she has the ability to compartmentalize this. You know opposites attract!) We were talking to banks for more than a year before it worked out. Eventually Leo had to take a job. He's still a director, but on an unpaid basis.

The banks struggle with us a little bit. Our deals are more troublesome than some because a person has to look at them, whereas 90 percent of their transactions are approved on a computer. But they're making money and they're pleased with it because our loan record is better than the bank's. Our low-income clients are paying their bills at a rate that's better than the average. And a lot of that has to do with our financial literacy program.

It's a win-win situation. I get people who come up and give me hugs, saying, "I never thought I could get out of debt." I believe that most individuals really want to do well. It's just that the system has built this circle around them that they can't escape. I personally think that the car contributes significantly to that circle. They don't understand credit. Poor people suffer more from that, but there are a lot of higher-income individuals who don't understand credit either, and what it does to our society today.

I want Bonnie CLAC to be successful, and I've worked harder than I would have liked on some occasions when it's gone through ups and downs financially. It's still not running on a self-sustaining basis, although we're getting closer every year. We're going to get there. I've been the key fund-raiser, but I'm not making too many trade-offs. I made a decision a long time ago that my family was very important, and I won't compromise that.

I'm an entrepreneur, and at some point you've got to get out of the entrepreneurial and into the procedural. I'm old enough and wise enough that I recognize some of my shortcomings. I'm not as enthusiastic about management as I can be about some things, and not that good at it. I'm also getting to be a little bit forgetful on some occasions. Now whether that's just plain age or just too much going on, I can't tell. I need people who can help me with that organizational aspect of the work.

I envision a chief operating officer running the organization in not too long, so I can focus on expansion and on policy. You can really affect a huge number of lives through this work, and I just need the time to be able to focus on doing that. If I put every one of those unscrupulous car dealers out of business, I'll be happy. They'll have to find ways to make more money off rich people, not just the poor.

CHAPTER THREE

The Perfect Storm

T he numbers are coming from the Census Bureau, but the metaphors are lifted straight from the Weather Channel.

For years, the surge of nearly 80 million baby boomers into the second half of life has been described as a great gray wave, moving inexorably forward, building in size and momentum with every passing day.

"We have a Category 5 financial hurricane on the horizon," Terry Savage announced breathlessly on the financial Web site TheStreet.com, "with barely Category 3 financial preparation on the part of individuals and the government to deal with this oncoming disaster." A *USA Today* headline proclaims the aging of the boomers a "fiscal hurricane." We face an "old age tsunami," declares Nicholas Eberstadt in an op-ed piece in the *Wall Street Journal*.

In *The Coming Generational Storm*, economist Lawrence Kotlikoff and journalist Scott Burns predict that by 2030, when "77 million baby boomers hobble into old age, walkers will outnumber strollers," leading to what the authors describe as "fiscal child abuse."

The unmistakable sign of heavy economic weather, say economists like Kotlikoff, is the increasingly unfavorable "age dependency ratio"—the number of working-age adults able to carry the burden for nonworking children, youth, and the elderly. That ratio has shrunk from 16 working-age adults per dependent when Social Security was established in 1935 to 3.3 workers per dependent today—and will shrink to 2 workers per dependent by 2030.

Atlantic Monthly writer Charles Mann bemoans "the coming death shortage." As aging boomers hit what has traditionally been considered "retirement age," these economists warn, the small population of working-age adults will bear the burden of supporting not only the truly needy but a burgeoning class of not-nearly-needy sixty- and seventy-somethings expecting to spend the second half of their adult lives in sustained leisure, damn the cost to other generations.

The consensus forecast: It's a disaster.

The metaphors of hurricanes, tsunamis, and other menacing storms and upheavals, natural and unnatural, conjure a battered society, under water, collapsed in ruins, all because its people are living longer, healthier lives.

But that makes no sense. How could the best thing that has ever happened to us as individuals—the dramatic extension of life and health—amount to the worst thing that has happened to us as a nation? How can the collective result of so much personal good fortune be national, or international, collapse?

The answer is that those apocalyptic forecasts are far from inevitable. We have a choice about our future, and the ability to create it. In the last century, a set of powerful economic and social forces combined to drive such a choice, and we invented the twentieth-century model of retirement. Now, another set of powerful trends is impelling us to formulate a different model.

Demographic and economic forces are intersecting with trends in longevity, the labor market, and human development to create new conditions, just at a time when social and environmental challenges call out for new approaches. Powerful forces are pushing Americans to work longer and in new ways, to use people's education and experience for higher purposes.

The one thing the forecasts do have right is the magnitude of the upcoming change, even if the shape of the change remains up for grabs. According to the United Nations, global aging, along with global warming and global terrorism, are the top three socioeconomic issues of the twenty-first century.

Such a perfect storm demands innovation and big thinking. As the late John Gardner, one of the great social innovators of the last century, often said, "What we have before us are breathtaking opportunities, disguised as insoluble problems."

Change Agents

In the twentieth century, economic and social conditions—from increases in longevity to Social Security to the need for jobs for young soldiers coming back from World War II—conspired to produce the need for a new vision of life after work. The Golden Years fit the need and the national mood like a glove. Today, another round of structural changes is rising to the surface, once again forcing the need for a new vision of the second half of life—and producing the opportunity to shape that vision.

INEXORABLE DEMOGRAPHICS. There are few things as inevitable as aging, so it's worth listening closely to the demographers.

In 2006, the first of nearly 76 million boomers turned sixty; every day now another 8,000 people join them. The wave will build through the 2020s, when the youngest boomers reach their sixties. Phrases such as the "Floridization of America" understate the scope of the generational transition underway. In Florida, the grayest (and most hurricane-prone) state, only 18 percent of residents today are over sixty; by 2030, nearly one in four of all the residents of the United States will have crossed that line.

And the United States is a youngster among advanced industrialized nations. In Japan, South Korea, Italy, Spain, and Germany, at least 40 percent of the populations will be sixty or older by midcentury. Even China, reaping an unintended consequence of its one-child policy, will have one in three people over sixty by 2050, a wild card that could derail its spectacular economic growth.

INCREASED LONGEVITY. *Twenty Good Years* was the title and premise of a mercifully short-lived sitcom that starred John Lithgow and Jeffrey Tambor as sixty-year-old buddies who vow to live every day as if it's their last. In fact, over the past century we've added more than thirty years to the average American life span, and improvements in health mean that for most people, most of those years are pretty good.

Most people who make it to the age of fifty can expect to live at least another thirty years, most of it in good health. For many, fifty is beginning to approximate the midpoint of their lives.

When Franklin Roosevelt signed the bill creating Social Security in 1935, the average sixty-five-year-old man could expect to live eleven or twelve more years; the sixty-five-year-old woman, fifteen more. Today, average sixty-five-year-olds are looking forward to 16.6 years for men, and 19.5 years for women. One-fourth of all Americans who turn sixty-five will see their ninetieth birthdays; by 2050, 40 percent of sixty-five-year-olds will be expected to reach ninety. According to the U.S. Census Bureau, by 2046 the number of people age 100 and over is expected to exceed 800,000, a tenfold increase over the number of centenarians currently alive.

Such increases in life expectancy can be expected to continue to increase. James Vaupel of the laboratory on longevity at Germany's Max Planck Institute shows that life expectancy has increased about 2.5 years per decade since 1840. "It's linear, absolutely linear, with no evidence of any decline or tapering off," he says, predicting that by midcentury *average* life expectancy in the longest-lived countries will exceed 100 years.

Just as important, the trend toward healthier aging continues. Researchers at Duke University's Center for Demographic Studies have shown an average annual decline in chronic disability of 1.7 percent for individuals sixty-five and older in the United States. Based on this calculus, the Duke team determined that the "active life expectancy," defined as the number of disability-free years an individual could expect at age sixty-five, was less than nine years in 1935, nearly twelve years by 1982, and is now approaching fourteen years—with projections that the period will increase to seventeen years in less than a decade.

Most individuals are no longer broken down physically by their midlife careers. The proportion of American workers today in jobs that are physically strenuous—requiring frequent lifting of objects weighing more than twenty-five pounds—had dropped to less than 8 percent by 1996, according to Urban Institute researchers Eugene Steuerle and Richard Johnson. They found a similar decline in the percentage of older workers who say that health problems interfere with their ability to do their jobs.

Long and healthy lives are in part the dividends of social investments in medical research and health care. Boomers' health concerns have helped drive a doubling of U.S. spending on health care since 1975, with one-third of the increase going to fight heart disease, lung disease, mental illness, cancer, and hypertension. As *Slate*'s Will Saletan writes, "The financial reward for that investment is that people can work later in life, paying taxes instead of collecting benefits. And they should."

FINANCIAL INSECURITY. Neither individual budgets nor the national budget can support three- or four-decade retirements.

Personal retirement planning used to be built on the assumption of five, ten, or fifteen years of life after work. With many boomers expected to live thirty or more years beyond traditional retirement age, it's a near certainty that old calculations will come up short. The ability to finance thirty years of traditional retirement is out of reach for all but the privileged few.

What's more, all three legs of the traditional stool of personal retirement financing are wobbly. Personal savings, company pensions, and Social Security are increasingly inadequate to the challenge ahead.

American families, like their government, are spending more than they take in. The personal savings rate, as a percentage of disposable income, has fallen from an average of more than 8 percent from the 1960s through the 1980s to below zero.

Even for those with some savings, the balances in most retirement accounts are woefully inadequate. A typical worker has just $60,000 in retirement savings, a balance that would produce a monthly check of less than $400 in retirement. Researchers at Boston College report that 43 percent of American households are unlikely to have enough money in retirement to reproduce their current lifestyle.

The notion of a secure and generous company-backed pension is as unusual as, well, the notion of a secure job itself. Firms are racing to shed their obligation to pay for both pensions and health-care coverage for their retirees. Whole industries, from airlines to autos, are dumping their pension obligations on the federal government, which will be able to pay retirees only a fraction of their promised benefits. Only one-third of all companies with more than 200 employees offer retiree health benefits today, down from two-thirds in 1988, according to the Kaiser Family Foundation.

Declares Alicia Munnell, director of Boston College's Center for Retirement Research: "Our employer-based social welfare system is collapsing."

Many Americans are ignorant, blissfully or otherwise, of

the inadequacy of their finances. The Employee Benefit Research Institute reports that most heads of household have no estimate of the money they will need to live comfortably in retirement.

ENDANGERED ENTITLEMENTS. Social Security is in no position to make up the difference for individual retirees.

Already, checks are getting smaller as a percentage of people's pre-retirement income, thanks to increases in Medicare premiums and taxes on benefits, plus a boost in the retirement age for full benefits, from sixty-five now to sixty-seven for people born in 1960 and later. More dramatic cuts in benefits are almost certainly in store, as policymakers belatedly tackle the huge bill for future Medicare and Social Security obligations.

Medicare is already running a cash deficit, and Social Security will start bleeding red ink in 2017. David Walker of the Government Accountability Office (GAO) calculates the total future liabilities of the U.S. government—that is, the funds it is committed to pay for Medicare, Social Security, interest on the debt, and other obligations—at $46.4 trillion, nearly equal to the total net worth of all households in the country. By the time the Social Security "trust fund" is exhausted in 2041, he says, the United States will have trouble paying any of its bills, not just Social Security checks.

Already, state spending on Medicaid has surpassed state education funding for the first time, and the gap is growing.

Rising costs are forcing us "to choose between care of our elderly and the education of our children," as Idaho governor Dirk Kempthorne told the 2005 White House Conference on Aging.

Politicians will debate the virtues of raising payroll taxes or cutting benefits for decades to come, but they will eventually return to an inescapable fact: Almost everyone will need to work longer or the system will collapse.

If most individuals work five additional years—delaying their benefits and continuing to make their payroll contributions and regular income tax payments—the projected 2045 Social Security deficit would more than disappear, according to researchers at the Urban Institute's Retirement Project. Boston College's Munnell shows that even two additional years of work—with people continuing to pay into the Social Security system instead of withdrawing—would go a long way to restoring the system's solvency.

Policymakers are likely to prod individuals to work longer by raising the eligibility age for collecting Social Security payments. The last major reform of Social Security, in 1983, included a gradual increase in the so-called normal retirement age, to sixty-seven for those born in 1960 or later. Social Security's trustees have evaluated a variety of proposals to increase the eligibility age for full benefits further, to sixty-eight. But as Will Saletan notes, that additional increase doesn't keep up with increases in life expectancy, even since 1983.

"If you were designing a system today" to cover the same

number of post-work years, Saletan writes, "you wouldn't set the retirement age at 65. You'd set it between 70 and 75." An increase to age seventy-three would cut the government's payout obligations by as much as 40 percent in 2050, eliminating the deficit and then some.

TALENT SHORTAGES. In a remarkable reversal, the flood of stories about older workers being tossed out with few opportunities is giving way to a new spate of coverage about the business imperative to retain and recruit older workers. The exit—and reentry—of baby boomers is creating confusing crosscurrents in the labor market.

As many as 64 million baby boomers (over 40 percent of the U.S. labor force) will start to reach "retirement age" by the end of this decade. And with a much smaller Generation X following the baby boomers, there will be fewer experienced workers to replace them. The number of workers age thirty-four to fifty-four in the United States is expected to grow by only 3 million in 2000–2020, down from a growth of 35 million in 1980–2000. As a result, one researcher puts the conservative estimate of the total U.S. labor shortage at nearly 9 million "full time equivalent" workers in 2010, and more than 18.1 million full-time workers in 2020.

In the same general time period, between 2007 and 2014, the number of workers fifty-five and older is expected to grow at a rate four times higher than the growth of the overall labor force, according to the Bureau of Labor Statistics.

There is a vigorous debate among experts about the scope of the impending talent and labor shortages, but there's little disagreement that some sectors are already feeling pinched. Industries already facing skill shortages include energy, health care, and government. Intel Corp., the semiconductor giant, has reported a shortage of people with advanced degrees in physics, chemistry, and engineering. Mercer, the large consulting firm, estimates between 20 and 25 percent of the roughly 2 million people in oil and gas refining, exploration, and production are or will soon be eligible for retirement.

The retirement wave is exacerbating long-standing shortages of teachers and nurses. The American Hospital Association this year found that 118,000 registered nurses were needed to fill vacancies at U.S. hospitals. By 2010, experts estimate a shortage of up to 1 million licensed practical nurses. With more than one-fifth of all public school teachers expected to be retired in five years, school districts around the country need an estimated 200,000 new teachers every year.

In the nonprofit sector, the aging of senior managers is feeding an unprecedented "leadership deficit," according to Bridgespan, a strategic consulting firm that works extensively with nonprofits. Bridgespan found that nonprofit organizations will need to attract and develop at least 330,000 and perhaps as many as 1 million new senior managers in the next ten years, quadrupling the number currently employed. By 2016, these organizations will need almost 80,000 new senior managers per year.

Baby boomers now nearing traditional retirement age represent a huge storehouse of such human capital, showcasing the extraordinary investments they, their parents, and society more broadly made in their education and training.

When boomers were just starting their careers, we couldn't build colleges and universities fast enough. Today more than 25 percent of boomers have a bachelor degree, compared to 15 percent of individuals already over age sixty-five. In the 1960s and 1970s, boomers drove tremendous growth in professional schools, particularly as women flocked into law school, medical school, business school, and other previously male-dominated fields. And boomers, women and men, never stopped going to school, swelling enrollment in all forms of continuing education.

In economic terms, the experience that people have in their jobs is an asset just like financial capital. In fact, in a knowledge economy, such human capital is perhaps more valuable than financial capital, since much of it is irreplaceable. Countless corporations in recent decades have discovered this too late, as they have purged their ranks of thousands of managers who once helped get things done.

SERIAL CAREERS. As lives have gotten longer, careers have gotten shorter. Indeed, serial careers of varying lengths are becoming the norm, not the exception. Boomers are simply extending the trend.

In the past, those who retired generally left the workforce for good. Today, the word "retirement" is losing its meaning, as boomers "retire" from their midlife careers but don't leave the workforce behind.

Some in the new fifty-five-plus workforce will simply stay at their current jobs longer. But others will be changing fields or even returning to work after a short hiatus. A study by Metlife found that the biggest reason those age sixty to sixty-five returned to work after "retiring" was to try something new. A second study, this one by Merrill Lynch, found that among baby boomers who expect to keep working, nearly two out of three expect to change fields.

Not all career transitions are voluntary, of course. Millions of U.S. workers in their fifties and sixties have been downsized, outsourced, replaced by offshore workers, bought out, eased out, or laid off. Many professions, from law to journalism, appear to have adopted their own versions of the navy's "thirty years and out," at least for those who don't make admiral.

For boomers whose midlife work has run its course, the question is no longer "What am I going to do for the next few years?" It's "What am I going to do for the next few decades?" For many, the answer will be not just another job, but another career, a new body of work.

PERSONAL HEALTH. Work used to be considered bad for people's health. No more.

Many jobs are indeed dangerous and physically ruinous over time. But there is increasing evidence today that extended work improves the psychological and physical health of people in the second half of life.

Social connections are a key to successful aging, according to a ten-year MacArthur Foundation study that found that lifestyle is more than twice as important as genes in determining whether individuals thrive late in life. Key ingredients of lifestyle, MacArthur researchers said, quoting Freud, are "love and work." Loving your work is doubly healthy, as it can provide strong social ties, a sense of purpose and contribution, a reason to get up in the morning, someplace to go, and an outlet for the productive impulse.

Such strong social connections, a key feature of work, are so important that researchers from the John F. Kennedy School of Government at Harvard describe them as "the health club of the 21st century."

A long-term study of nuns found that the women were not only particularly long-lived but remarkably resistant to Alzheimer's disease. Dr. David Snowdon, a neurology professor at the University of Kentucky Medical School, found that the nuns' strong sense of community, the social ties of working with other nuns and with young people contributed to their health and longevity. "That love of other people, that caring, how good they are to each other and patient, that's something all of us can do," he said.

Other researchers have found that tutoring elementary school students in reading can slow aging. Researchers at Johns Hopkins University Medical Centers randomly separated two groups of older adults—half became members of

Experience Corps and worked fifteen hours per week helping Baltimore schoolchildren learn to read. The other half served as a control group, not working at all. Researchers found that "physical, cognitive, and social activity" increased significantly for Experience Corps members, while decreasing for those in the control group.

Study after study suggests work may be a fountain of youth and retirement the opposite. A study in Jerusalem of 1,000 men and women born in 1920 found that those who continued to work at the age of seventy and beyond were 2.5 times more likely to be alive at the age of eighty-two than those who had retired. "I tell people, 'You invest your savings into this and that, but there is something else you can do that is a big investment in your health,'" Dr. Yoram Maaravi of Hadassah Hospital Mt. Scopus told the *Wall Street Journal*. "If you put the effort into finding work that is meaningful, you are gaining life."

"There seem to be health benefits to keeping all of your body parts moving—including the nerve cells in your brain," says John Trojanowski, director of the University of Pennsylvania Institute on Aging. "And the more engaged you are with other people, the more healthy you are."

WORK AND MEANING. Human development doesn't end with adulthood. Later years bring changes that increase the desire of many for meaningful roles, particularly work that lets them pass on what they know to others.

William James understood this. "The great use of life," he said, "is to spend it for something that will outlast us." Psychologists call this stage generativity. Erik Erikson defines generativity as the realization that an essential responsibility of human life is to pass on what we have learned to future generations; as he put it, "I am what survives of me."

Drawing on Erikson's work, Harvard Medical School professor and researcher George Vaillant positions generativity after the central midlife work of career consolidation and says it springs from the realization that time is not endless, that eventually there will come a period of decline and then death itself.

Vaillant argues that generativity after the career consolidation phase "means community building," including mentoring and coaching younger generations. In longitudinal research across individuals from a wide range of backgrounds, he found that those who mastered community building were emotionally happier and healthier. "In all three study cohorts," he writes, "mastery of generativity tripled the chances that the decade of the seventies would be for these men and women a time of joy and not despair."

Of course, boomers' search for meaningful work is nothing new. From the time they stormed onto the scene, most boomers have approached work with a determination to make it more than a paycheck. "They expect in some sense that their careers will help them realize their authentic self," says Harvard political scientist Russell Muirhead, author of *Just Work.*

A survey by Smith Barney concluded that tens of millions

of boomers want to remain active in the workforce, value community, shun materialism for "experiences"—and feel something is missing from their lives. Three out of five "welcome more novelty and change." More than twice as many value being "a leader in the community" more than having an expensive car.

Although boomers will work longer for many reasons—to earn money, stay healthy, maintain social connections, feel accomplished, keep busy, maintain identity—in the end, the real force driving people to find *meaningful* work is not economic or social, but personal. It's that inner voice calling for something as simple as a change of pace, as ambitious as changing the world, as profound as reclaiming a dream deferred before it is denied.

Never Retire

We're approaching a turning point as increasing numbers of people eschew traditional retirement for something very different. Stories of social-purpose second careers have become staples of such magazines as *More* and Oprah Winfrey's magazine, *O*, targeted to women in midlife, and are at the core of new magazines, aiming at a boomer audience, such as *What's Next* and *Motto*. The latter magazine's mission statement: "We believe it's impossible to have a meaningful life without meaningful work. So, we created the first media company for

people seeking a more personally fulfilling and socially responsible route to business success."

The first four segments of *NBC Nightly News's American
Boomers* series, launched in conjunction with the first
boomers' turning sixty in 2006, featured second acts in
good-work jobs. These profiles included doctors who had
switched from private practice to working in free clinics, Experience Corps members who were working in schools, an
Avon executive who moved to lead Girls Inc. in her mid-
fifties, and another woman who had left the business world
to move into a management role at Goodwill.

According to an *NBC News* script, "It used to be you'd
collect your pension and whatever toys you could afford . . .
and exit the workforce. But that model's fading away." The
last line in NBC's script was left to advertising executive
Dick Tarlow: "I've got, what, ten good years left?" asks Tarlow. "Why not use 'em to help other people?"

In its June 2006 issue, *U.S. News and World Report* ran a
cover story arguing against retirement. Among the reasons it
cites are the many benefits of work and the opportunity to
do work that matters to the larger community. As the article
notes, "Financial concerns may be the first reasons older
workers offer to explain why they're staying on the job, but
researchers have found that one deeper reason—the need to
make a meaningful contribution—is often the more important motivating factor."

One of the most eloquent testimonials to the new normal
came from William Safire, former speechwriter for Richard

Nixon and author of more than 3,000 columns for the *New York Times*. At seventy-five, Safire had good health, high spirits, and lots more to say. And he had long valued the counsel of Nobel laureate and DNA co-discoverer James Watson, who told him, "Never retire. Your brain needs exercise or it will atrophy." So why would he leave his *Times* column (he kept his Sunday magazine column on language), one of the best soapboxes in America?

Safire explained in his final column in 2005, which opened with the words, "Here's why I'm outta here." The legendary adman Bruce Barton had advised Safire fifty years earlier to keep trying new things. "When you're through changing, you're through," is now widely attributed to Barton, though Safire now claims to have coined it himself.

"Combine those two bits of counsel—never retire, but plan to change your career to keep your synapses snapping—and you can see the path I'm now taking," Safire wrote. He advised, "Retraining and fresh stimulation are what all of us should require in 'the last of life, for which the first was made.'"

Readers, he cautioned, should think about their longevity strategy. While policymakers debate about Social Security, people should be planning their own "social activity" accounts, he said. "Intellectual renewal is not a vast new government program, and to secure continuing social interaction deepens no deficit."

The key, Safire wrote, is starting early. "By laying the basis for future activities in the midst of current careers, we reject stultifying retirement and seize the opportunity for an exhilarating second wind."

Safire himself left the *Times* to take a full-time job leading the nonprofit Dana Foundation, which focuses on brain research, immunology, and public health education. For him, this next step offered a chance to go deep on one issue, after a career of going wide on many. His experience as a polemicist, as he put it, made it easier to wade into public controversies over science and ethics.

The first controversy he waded into was over the nature of the new stage of life between midlife and old age. We've added thirty years to life, extending longevity from forty-seven to seventy-seven over the past century, he wrote, with the likelihood of significant further extensions. "But to what purpose?" Safire asks. "If the body sticks around while the brain wanders off, a longer lifetime becomes a burden on self and society. Extending the life of the body gains most meaning when we preserve the life of the mind."

Safire revised Barton's advice once again: "When you're through changing, learning, working to stay involved—only then are you through." But he closed by quoting Watson again: "Never retire."

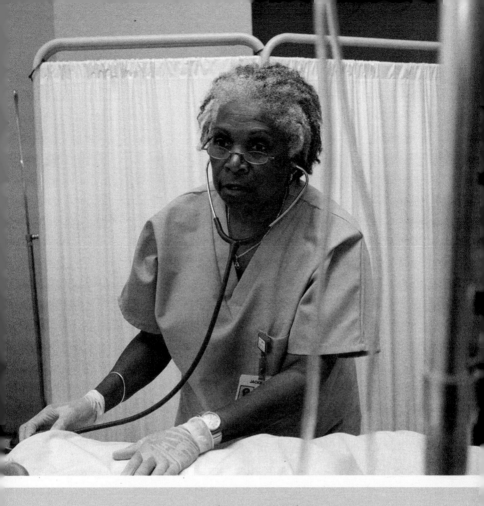

Jacqueline Khan

Truant Officer
to Critical Care Nurse

was in my early fifties when I decided to go into nursing. I never wanted to work in a job for thirty years, though I stayed with the Detroit Board of Education for that long. I was a truant officer, investigating why students were not attending school. I liked it but didn't think I could learn any more after fifteen or twenty years. I was sort of a coward: I wanted to have a pension, and I wanted to have health care. I could have left years before, but I didn't. I waited until I knew that I would be secure financially.

But while I was working, I got a two-year associate's degree in nursing. I officially retired from the Board of Education on February 1, 1999, but I had already started my regular nursing classes the week before. It was quite intense. I loved it. I then got my Bachelor of Science degree in nursing.

I'm a critical care nurse and I work at the Level One trauma hospital in Detroit, primarily in cardiac intensive care. I have twelve-hour shifts and the hardest thing about work for me has always been getting up and getting there. Once I'm there, with the help of a couple of espressos, I can stay there a long time. Twelve hours is really not bad.

I want my work to be difficult so I can keep my mind sharp and stay physically fit and all of that. I've been offered jobs in telephone triage, where you sit next to your telephone and talk to people. Inside of me is a person who wants to sit down and eat potato chips, so I couldn't be in a situation in which that person emerged. I'm not interested in that. I'm going to live my life until it's over. I'm not going to just sit around.

I do this for the excitement. I like drama. I like health. I want to be healthy. I don't want to spend my remaining years on this planet not well. When you see the things people are dealing with, this thing just keeps playing in your mind: *Keep it together, keep it together!* In nursing you have to be up to the challenge all the time. You have to be strong, to be able to turn patients over and help them stand up.

I know if you don't keep your mind active, a lot of things go. At sixty-four, I really do not think that my life is over; it's still evolving and beginning. I want to have an opportunity to do something new and different every day if I can, and to be involved in something that keeps my mind active, to be with other people who are knowledgeable, with whom you share information, to watch other people work and to have something to do.

I think I make a direct impact. First of all, I'm an older nurse, and I look like an older nurse. My hair is as gray as it is black. I was taking care of a lady who was seventy-three, quite a nice lady. She was really in quite bad condition. In addition to congestive heart failure, she was unable to stand unassisted. She was an independent person, so this made it sort of rough for her. She was unable to take care of any of her physical needs. So I bathed her and cleaned her up, and she said to me, "You know I think you're sort of like me." And I said, "What do you mean?" And she said, "You know how important it is to be cleaned up, have yourself cleaned up and have your teeth brushed before you eat." We understood each other. And when I with my gray hair said, "Come on now, I need you to sit on the side of the bed," she was looking at me thinking she could probably do it. It's not that someone twenty-two couldn't have had the same effect, but I think it was easier for me. That's really gratifying to me. It's better than any paycheck.

Oftentimes in hospital work, things are very controversial, especially when people are sick and the family comes in. I had a very touching case of a young lady who was twenty-three, who looked like she was fifteen, who had come into the hospital on an emergency. She was unconscious. She had had an asthma attack at a bar and apparently was down for some time before she was transported by the emergency vehicles. Because her heart was not doing what it should, oxygen was not circulating, so she was experiencing brain damage. By the time she got up to the floor, she was brain damaged. They hadn't really declared it, but she was. They hadn't told her mother.

Mom had gone home to take a bath and change clothes so she could come back. She had no idea and comes back and asks how her daughter's doing. I have a little thing that I say, "She's not doing as well as we'd like for her to be doing right now." People accept that—I'm always stunned because I wouldn't accept that! But people just say, "Oh, okay. But you're working on her?" And I can actually say yes because you can see that I'm working.

I go out to the doctor and say, "Does Mom understand the condition of the daughter? Because she's asking me if she can spend the night in case she needs anything." He tells me they told her in the emergency room. I ask what they told her in ER. He tells me they told her she was brain damaged. I say, "Do you think she knows what that means? How brain damaged is she? Does that mean she can't see out of one eye?" He tells me that it's the brain stem, which means she's through. It's over. She's twenty-three and looks fifteen and she's going to die. So I ask, "Does Mom know this?" The doctors don't say much. I tell them they're going to have to tell her. It's inhumane for her not to realize that her twenty-three-year old child is alive only because of the machines. She has a right to know.

They don't want to tell her, so I go back in and Mom tells me she saw me talking to the doctors. She asks if anything's changed, and I say no. I just stay in the room with her. I knew that she would finally ask me, "What should I do?" I tell her, "I can't tell you what to do, but I'll tell you what I would do. I would go out and ask for the doctor in charge. And I'd ask what the diagnosis and prognosis is. The diagnosis will tell you what is exactly wrong with your daughter and the prognosis will tell you if she's going to get well."

She did, and the doctor came in and he did a very good job. He didn't want to, but he was forced into service, and he did a very good job of explaining to her and he put it in terms that she could understand. He had to say to her that her daughter's brain is so damaged that it's not running the body's systems. And when he told her that, she got it. She knew. She handled it well. She knew. She called her other family members in. She asked if we had a chaplain. She knew.

That kind of experience makes you grateful. It makes you realize that life is short and time is fleeting, and do it your way. Don't have these artificial constraints and don't wake up to say, "Well I'm sixty-four so I can't do this and I can't do that." If you want to learn to Rollerblade, you should do it. When you work in a situation in which people die, a lot, then it makes life more important. And it makes little trivial things just exactly that—annoying and trivial.

Working in a hospital and seeing death a lot and having to do postmortem care, you see that one second you're alive and the next you're gone, and you can tell. It's like the soul or whatever that is really departs, and you realize that you're only looking at an empty something there. That essence that made that a person is gone. It makes you think about life: What have you done to make life better for yourself, for others? Have you made someone smile? Have you shown you care? Because it's going to come to this for all of us. It makes you, I don't know, more relaxed in a way.

The most important thing that I've learned in my whole life is that in life you really have to do exactly what it is that you wish to do, within reason. If you have a goal—a book to write or a job to do—you should do it. All of this business that we learned when we were young people, like "Life doesn't last forever," "Tomorrow isn't promised"—all of that stuff that just goes right over your head when you're in your twenties and thirties, but it's all true. My favorite song now is the song by Frank Sinatra about doing it his way. A lot of people won't agree with that. But in life, I think the important thing is to do something for others and something for yourself and something for the planet and move on.

Our society until recently saw retirement age as a time when you just retired from life. You just sort of went away, and that's what most people looked forward to, or at least they thought they were looking forward to it. In recent years I think that there has been more emphasis on being a total person, a well-rounded person. I think your post-retirement interests are things that you really, really like because you don't have to do it if you don't want to. If you work after retirement, you do it on your own terms.

I don't think there are that many obstacles to continuing to work. A lot of people who are sixty-five and older work and could do even more work, could have their own businesses, could do whatever. There's a brain trust there. There's a lot of good information there. You start off here, and you do this and you do that, and you practice, and after a while you're doing it. I think people just don't realize that they could do it. Once they take the ball, they'll run away with it. And then they start to do more of those things and they bring out all of those things inside of them that have been there all the time, but for some other reason, for whatever reason, they weren't a priority.

And people get so sad. We have to stop getting so sad as a group, and by that I mean a lot of times at sixty, sixty-five, you've had deaths of people of who are really, really, really important to you. You just allow yourself to become overwhelmed with sadness—it's a constant temptation. You have to fight that and then you have to find something to put in its place. You can still be sad part-time, but you don't have to be sad full-time.

I don't think about quitting. My plan is to never retire. Once I've done something or learned something, I want to do something more exciting. I keep my eye on those Doctors Without Borders. I think I have the physical stamina to do it, to go to lots of different countries. I wouldn't mind going to some of these countries and having an entirely different lifestyle. You know, I am accustomed to certain trappings, and I say that I'm not interested in these trappings. Well, let's put up or shut up. Let's go and see.

I sold my car today. It was a 2003 black Ford Taurus, with black leather seats, sunroof, the whole thing. It was perfect. It was an older lady's car; it was a car that was a nice, substantial, well-built, medium-sized, medium-priced car. So, I was so happy I sold it today because I want an Element. The Element is very retro to me because it reminds me of the Volkswagen Thing which was big when I was youthful. You can throw your gym shoes in there, you can throw plants in there, you can pack in there, you can throw anything you want and off you go. It's a strange color. It's a strange shape. It's wonderful.

It's sort of symbolic of where I'm going. When I got the Ford, I needed it because a person very close to me was ill and so we were going back to New York to Sloan-Kettering. That's when I got that car, so that he would be comfortable on the trip. Now, I'm going to get rid of that car. I'm not getting rid of my feelings for my significant other; I'm not getting rid of my thoughts for him or anything, but I'm getting rid of this car. That's not where I am now.

It's so easy to allow yourself to say, "Oh, I don't feel good today, I have to rest." I think it was Malcolm X who said you can rest when you're dead. I feel that way.

CHAPTER FOUR

A Fresh Map of Life

rank Reece scored big in the soaring telecommuni-
cations industry of the 1990s. He built his own
equipment sales and service company, U.S. Telecen-
ters, and took it from a small New England service provider
to a nationwide sales network, then sold it near the top of an
overheated market. He and his wife raised two kids in a
comfortable house in Cambridge, Massachusetts.

Then a succession of shocks knocked loose Reece's moor-
ings. His next venture, a communications company, didn't
survive the dot-com bust, leaving his midlife career a combination of "modest success and spectacular failure." In quick
succession, his mother died, his business died, then he nearly
died himself after rupturing his Achilles tendon on Thanks-

giving Day 2001. The injury led to blood clots in his leg and a series of pulmonary embolisms, requiring months of convalescence and rehabilitation. "There was a certain sense of financial achievement that I was after," he says, "and I practically killed myself pursuing it."

At fifty-five, the athletic overachiever found himself wandering in a fog. "If you've ever sailed in the fog, you know you're pretty well lost," he says. "And if you don't know where you are, you don't know where you're going. I was adrift. I didn't have any landmarks that were familiar to me."

At home alone during the workday for the first time, he felt isolated, "pretending to work" with only his computer and his telephone. "When you close the book on one career and you haven't opened the book on another, there is a sense of regret, loss, a confusion about what to do," he says. "I didn't know how to label myself," he says. "I didn't know what to put on a business card."

The fog lasted several years. Reece's journey was more an uneasy bend toward a new direction than a dramatic turning point. *I've got thirty more years to live,* he remembers saying to himself. *I'm not going to play golf. I missed my shot at the pro tour! So how do I want to excel for the next thirty years?*

At the time, Reece served on the board of a nonprofit organization he'd helped to found years earlier. With its goal of instilling environmental values in youth, the Global Habitat Project helped high school students produce *Greentimes,* a newsletter distributed to middle and elementary school classrooms in inner-city schools four times a year, reaching

30,000 young readers. In 2004, when the organization was looking for a new executive director, Reece put his hand up.

It wasn't just a new sense of direction that Reece was after, but also some balance. "I thought that the nonprofit arena might be a little calmer," he says. "As it turns out, it's not actually calmer, but that's okay," he says. "When I was in business, I actually made money. Now that I'm in a non-profit, I beg for money."

Reece says that he is still ambitious, but his metrics for success have changed. "I want to reach more teachers and more children, and I'd like to roll up this organization and then roll it out to more communities," he says, adding, "I don't need to be world famous. I just need to reach more children."

The Next Chapter

Reece and millions of others are on the front end of an enormous social transformation.

Neither young nor old, they are closing a chapter in their lives and their work, yet stand decades away from anything resembling traditional old age. They face not only the question of what's next, but who they are now. Betty Friedan, writing about women seeking a new identity in the early 1960s, talked about the problem that has no name; this is the population with no name. Are they seniors, elders, retirees?

Address them as such and they will refer you to their parents. Lurching forward, they head down a path poorly labeled, with only rudimentary road maps, an array of pitfalls, and few rites of passage. It is little surprise that when a recent survey by Thrivent Lutheran Services, a nonprofit financial services provider, asked leading-edge boomers to select the song that best described this period, they chose "The Long and Winding Road."

Even the accepted wisdom today is misleading. It has become commonplace to hear that boomers are reinventing retirement. But the unfolding transformation goes well beyond even that more expansive definition of an established institution, beyond reinventing, revolutionizing, or redefining retirement. It goes beyond retirement itself.

The word *retirement*—derived from the old French *retirer*, to go off into seclusion—hardly applies to the period boomers are now entering. Individuals will surely continue to retire; they'll just do so much later, and in a more contemporary style. Think yoga classes instead of shuffleboard courts. And think seventy-five- or eighty-year-olds, who are in much the same place in terms of physical health and life expectancy as the sixty- and sixty-five-year-olds of an earlier era. Rather than being reinvented, retirement as we have known it is being deferred and displaced.

The important story is that something new is being *invented*. We are in the midst of fashioning a new stage of life between the traditional midlife years and careers, and true retirement and old age. It is a development that is distinct, significant, and historic. It is a mistake to see it as more of midlife as we know it, an updated version of retirement, or the new old age. It is what it is, and, most of all, what we make of it. It is big: as long as midlife, decades in duration. And it is uncertain, as the population explosion among those entering this work in progress means tens of millions of boomers find themselves navigating uncharted territory.

Fifty years ago, millions deemed too old to work, too young to die were the raw material for the creation of the Golden Years. In the postwar period, the structural forces establishing modern retirement were in place, but the meaning of the new arrangements remained undeveloped. The financial services industry and the developers swooped in to provide that meaning. In a remarkably brief period of time, using extraordinary creativity and entrepreneurship, combining marketing savvy and the ability to create large-scale new vehicles for people to act on the dreams they were peddling, they created a reality so powerful that it seemed as though it had always been there.

Now that the Golden Years are looking tarnished, the confusion about what's next is even deeper. One tiny but telling sign: The original Leisure World in Orange County, California, decided to change its name to Laguna Woods Village in 2005. Marty Rhodes, chairman of the name-change committee, explained that they hope to change "the connotation . . . that we're old doddering people in walkers and wheelchairs . . . waiting for the grim reaper."

Even as the boomers move into their next chapter, the

meaning of these new arrangements remains unclear. Many don't even know how to conceive of their age. In a recent survey of 500 sixty-year-olds, 40 percent said "60 is the new 50" and 28 percent said "60 is the new 40." AARP's magazine—the largest-circulation publication in the country— even suggested sixty might be the new thirty, with a photo of the forever-young Lauren Hutton on the cover. The possibility that sixty might be *the new sixty* appears not to merit consideration.

Similarly, the fact that we can't even figure out what to call people reflects a broader vacuum in meanings and expectations. When *Parade* magazine in 2006 sponsored a contest to come up with a new label for the post-sixty stage of life, 4,000 responses poured in. The results were less than inspiring. "Seasoned citizens," suggested fifty-two-year-old Cynthia Solaka from Charlotte, North Carolina. LeAnne Reaves, fifty-seven, of Hurst, Texas, nominated "OWLS," for older, wiser, livelier souls. Others suggested such uncomfortable neologisms as "geri-actives." It is as if the contest goal had been to rename the oldest-old.

Others have suggested "second act," "third phase," "zoomers," the "third quarter," the "new old" and the "well-derly" (as opposed to the "ill-derly"). The linguist Geoffrey Nunberg himself has added the word "gerries" to the pile, picking it up from a twenty-something New Yorker en route to Florida to see his grandmother, who used it as shorthand for "geriatrics." The National Center for Health Statistics characterizes individuals in the age group fifty-five to sixty-four as the "near elderly." For good reason, perhaps, none of the terms has stuck.

It is easy to lampoon our failure of imagination thus far. But it takes time to establish the trappings of a new stage of life, including the very name of that stage, the people who inhabit it, and the lifestyle they embody. We invent these stages in the United States perhaps once a century. Prior to the early twentieth century, for example, adolescence scarcely existed as a category. A proliferation of young people who were neither children nor exactly adults led to the creation of the American adolescent, or as they came to be known, teenagers. A century earlier, we had little sense of childhood; we dressed young people as little adults and expected them to act that way.

The New Crown of Life

One of the first to recognize the scope and significance of the newest such stage was British historian Peter Laslett, who twenty years ago published *A Fresh Map of Life: The Emergence of the Third Age*. It is arguably the single most important book published on the changes unfolding in front of us, perhaps because it sprang from the mind of a social scientist accustomed to observing the wide sweep of human events, to discerning the patterns only visible in the long view.

In *A Fresh Map of Life*, first published in England, then

adapted for the United States in the late 1980s, Laslett challenges us to recognize that we live in "a world entirely unknown to all previous Americans," one that defies the widely accepted progression of childhood to adulthood to old age to the great beyond, with a stop in retirement along the way. The new combination of longevity and demographics, he argues, means everyone needs "an intelligible guide to a social landscape which otherwise we shall never understand."

Laslett's new map of life is built around the emergence of what he called the "third age," which follows the first age of childhood and adolescence and the second of child rearing and midlife careers, but precedes the fourth age—the time of frailty and decline. Defying conventional wisdom, Laslett views the development of the third age as an individual and societal triumph, "the crown of life." At the heart of his thinking is the simple insight that individuals at this juncture have, for a protracted period and in large numbers, both experience and time.

These insights came not only from the perspective of a historian but from the personal experience of a "third ager." As Laslett reached his seventies, he became interested in growing older and in the transformation of the period beyond midlife. He was adamant that the third age was not fixed chronologically, railing against attempts to peg it at fifty to seventy-four (he was eighty-one at the time; he died in 2001 at eighty-five). He regarded *A Fresh Map of Life* as a call to liberate one-fifth of the population "for that self-fulfillment which the years of added life make possible for everyone." Yet the realization of this prospect, available for the first time in human history, he said, would require two forms of liberation: one in our thinking, the next in action.

Laslett himself plunged forward on both fronts, not only through his writing and advocacy but by becoming a social entrepreneur—in cahoots with Michael Young, one of the great innovators of his generation in England. In his earlier days, Young invented the concept of meritocracy, authored the postwar platform of the Labour Party, and wrote brilliantly and prolifically. In his eighties, he created The School for Social Entrepreneurs in London. In between, he started the Open University with Laslett and others, and with Laslett again, the University of the Third Age. Involving hundreds of thousands, the U3A made lifelong learning a reality in England.

Some thoughtful commentators in America have taken up Laslett's call for new thinking. *Washington Post* columnist Abigail Trafford writes about the emergence of "middle-escence." Former *Ms.* magazine editor Suzanne Braun Levine suggests what we're seeing is "second adulthood." George Washington University researcher and psychiatrist Gene Cohen calls the phenomenon the "second half of life." And Professor Phyllis Moen of the University of Minnesota, one of the most astute observers of the changing life course, articulates a theory of "midcourse," including room for a "midcourse correction."

Shoshana Zuboff of Harvard Business School laid out a schema of "The New New Adulthood" in 2004. "The first half of life is about compulsion; the second half is about choice," Zuboff writes. "Nature compels physical and cognitive maturation through early adulthood. Then the need to earn a place in society kicks in: education, career, family, status, recognition, and achievement." Once those were over and done with, she observes, "it used to be time to die."

In the new arrangement, Zuboff concludes, "decades stretch ahead. Some people, to be sure, simply continue their youthful MO, without much reflection. But for many, the old incentives no longer bite. They find themselves feeling uneasy."

Unwilling to simply observe emerging patterns, Zuboff, like Laslett, turned to social innovation directly, helping to create Harvard's Odyssey Program, dubbed "School for the Second Half of Life." She notes that for the program's participants, "just because they are grown-ups doesn't mean that they are finished growing up." Where consumer products companies see a market of 100 million Americans over forty-five to whom they can peddle skin creams, fitness equipment, and vitamins, and where governments see fiscal problems on a massive scale, Zuboff sees "a nation of fellow pilgrims, embarking on a whole new adventure in being human."

Turning Points

Steve Weiner had an illustrious career in higher education, capped when he became the provost of Mills College in Oakland, California, and headed the commission that accredits colleges and universities in California and other Western states. At fifty-five, while on a three-month sabbatical in New Zealand with his wife, he came to the conclusion that his midlife career had run its course. Once home, he told the chairman of the accreditation commission that he was planning to retire in two years.

When the time came, Weiner felt liberated—from alarm clocks, from carrying work home on weekends, from "the burden of ambitions" he had long carried on his shoulders. Actuarial tables showed him there was a good likelihood he would live another thirty years, and he was confident his finances would hold out. After decades of long hours, Weiner accepted his new "retired" status and described himself as "vocationally celibate."

Six months later, Weiner felt discontent, frustrated, and eager for change. He had assumed he'd sit on nonprofit boards and perhaps do some consulting. And he was able to do all of that, including some volunteer work. But retirement was beginning to feel like "the weekend that never ends," as a friend called it, and Weiner was ready for something significant. "I actively struggle with what it means to be successful in retirement," he reflected. "I would like to have at least one more passionate involvement in something I care about deeply."

Weiner cared about college opportunity for all. He remembered back to 1960, when the state of California adopted the Master Plan for Higher Education, a promise that every qualified student wishing to pursue a college education would have access to a public college or university—and he knew that that promise was in jeopardy. Today, the number of young people of college-going age is skyrocketing, but the capacity of the state's public community colleges and universities is not increasing accordingly.

Weiner decided to take action. With David Wolf, a "retired" community college president, he created the Campaign for College Opportunity, a nonprofit advocacy group devoted to ensuring that the next generation of college-age students in California has the chance to go to college as promised. Armed with a timely and compelling idea, they raised millions of dollars from such institutions as the Rockefeller and Hewlett Foundations, even though neither Wolf nor Weiner had ever done that kind of fund-raising before. They hired a diverse staff composed largely of dynamic young people. And they brought together a bipartisan coalition that included groups that had never worked together before, ranging from the California Business Roundtable to the Mexican-American Legal Defense and Education Fund.

Then they started all over again, creating Common Sense California, hoping to rejuvenate civic action and sensible policymaking in their home state. For Weiner, the work constitutes "the single most satisfying professional experience of his career." Equally powerful, from the perspective of generativity, much of this work is dedicated to a future that neither Weiner nor Wolf will ever see, even with the benefits of longevity.

Weiner's "false" retirement—in contrast to the "true" retirement that will still come later for many—illuminates a key feature of the emerging new stage of life. What at first may look like, and even feel like, retirement, often turns out to be a sabbatical, a rest stop, the chance to travel, to spend time with friends and family, to take a break before moving on to the next phase of engagement.

An ad for Aetna reflects this emerging trajectory. As a girl swings dreamily beneath a tree, the ad invites consumers to dream along by filling in the blanks. "When I was a kid I wanted to be a _____," the ad begins. "But life kind of got in the way and I grew up and became a _____. So when I retire I'm going to do what I always wanted to do and _____. But first I want to jump on a plane and see _____. And maybe take my family to _____. Then I'll get down to business."

Like Aetna's protagonist, Weiner's retirement hiatus was a temporary transition, more prelude than destination. And it was a needed rest: After years of climbing the career ladder, he was exhausted. He's not the only one. Midlife overwork has reached pathological proportions in this country. The International Labor Organization reports that Americans added thirty-six hours of work per year on average during the 1990s, bringing the annual total to forty-nine and one-half weeks of work. That catapulted Americans into the lead as the most overworked population on the planet, easily taking over the title long held by Japanese workers. The situation is even more dire for women juggling what sociologist Arlie Hochschild calls the second shift—long hours both at work and at home.

After his sabbatical served its purpose, Weiner simply "un-retired," joining 7 million other Americans who have returned to work after "retiring," according to Putnam Investment. Putnam estimated about twice as many of the un-retired "want to work" rather than "have to work." But the truth is that, for many, both aspects are present and powerful and the result is the same: They will work.

Fatigue is only one of the reasons for such a hiatus. There is also the question of what comes next, and the truth that the busyness and other challenges of the first half of adulthood crowd out much time to think about, much less test out, answers to such questions. So, many end up at a point, usually in their fifties, when they need both time to rest and the chance to contemplate new directions.

"A growing number of mid-career professionals are at a crossroads, stuck in jobs they've lost passion for," says Herminia Ibarra, a management professor at INSEAD in France, and author of the book *Working Identity*. "They don't know what they want to do and who they want to be."

"Adulthood simply goes on too long without punctuation," argues cultural anthropologist Mary Catherine Bateson, adding: "The famous midlife crisis is a search for that punctuation, for the feeling that one is making a new start." We expect life to unfold in "a familiar rhythm of preparation and achievement, arrivals and departures, excitement and quiescence," Bateson wrote in the *Harvard Business Review* in 2005. "But our mental model of these stages and transitions is fast becoming outdated."

Making a similar point, a *Time* magazine cover story in 2005 heralded the emergence of a female midlife crisis, as more and more women pause to reassess where they are headed. With the life span stretching, "There is room for multiple midlife crises," *Time* noted, suggesting a "quarter-life crisis" at twenty-five, the traditional one at forty, and a third one occurring twenty years later. "We are living too long and too well to stay settled even in a contented state for more than a few years at a time," the article states, concluding: "And with experience, each new life-cycle crisis stands a better chance of looking like just another chance to start all over again."

Further feeding this trend is compression in the span of many careers, just as life spans continue to grow. Legal careers, for example, are becoming much like the military career—twenty or twenty-five years and out. According to professor Marc Galanter of the University of Wisconsin, competitive pressures encourage younger partners to force out older colleagues. In journalism, as in the auto industry, the "buyout" has become an increasingly familiar part of the landscape for individuals in their forties and fifties. More than one in five Americans are forced to retire from their midlife career earlier than planned, as a result of layoffs, downsizing, personal illness, or injury, according to a survey by Sun Life Financial.

The end of a career is less likely to be marked by a formal

retirement like Steve Weiner's, and more likely to be a murky mixture of signals that it's time to move on: a downsizing, a layoff, a buyout. Sometimes, it just becomes clear that enough is enough and it's time to take the next step in the life journey. And sometimes it is a true crisis: Frank Reece never had a retirement party, only a business failure and health collapse that drove home the truth that his midlife career had run its course.

Psychologists have long advised that major life changes—the loss of a job, the death of a parent or spouse or child, a serious illness or divorce, even moving to a new area—deliver powerful shocks to the system, often precipitating depression and disorientation. And shocks, disorientation, and confusion often accompany the end of what could be called the first half of adulthood. With 41 million baby boomers now between fifty-one and sixty years old, such individual transitions are gathering into a major social phenomenon.

These instances of personal upheaval are more than a matter of psychology, of individuals finding their footing. They are magnified many times by the reality of unsettled social and cultural institutions—of individuals coming of age at a juncture when old norms, pathways, and policies have collapsed and new ones are just beginning to take shape.

Shifting Visions

As we have seen, financial services firms are already waging campaigns to define the meaning of the new stage of life. The same firms that shaped the last generation of later-life dreams are now investing billions in research and marketing in an attempt to brand themselves as the managers of choice for the boomers' trillions in financial assets. The expensive ad campaigns rolled out in recent years by banks, brokerages, and insurance companies show which psychological chords their studies have encouraged them to pluck.

These visions are sometimes contradictory, and occasionally retrograde, but they also tap powerful aspirations for the period of life where retirement once stood. Financial marketers are working hard to sell individuals something to look forward to, a vision of their future that is powerful enough for them to defer consumption in the first half of adulthood in order to invest in their aspirations for the second half. Retirement issues of personal finance magazines, stocked with advertising from the financial services industry, carry articles that trumpet the satisfaction of individuals who are living fulfilling lives in their fifties, sixties, and beyond.

Ameriprise, for example, appeals to the quintessentially American fantasy of reinvention. "Dictionary definition of re-tire-ment: 1. To disappear 2. To go away 3. To withdraw. *Our* definition of retirement: 1. To be connected 2. To reinvent 3. Freedom."

Lincoln Financial offers its own menu of possibilities.

"Maybe you'll finish your life's work early. Maybe your next retirement party won't be your last. Maybe all a gold watch tells you is the time. Maybe you prefer your days to be filled with challenge and passion and purpose. Maybe today is the day you wake up and say . . . Hello, Future."

Going beyond advertising, financial services providers are offering life coaching through their financial advisers. Ameriprise found that boomers consider having "a financial adviser who understands what is important to them" as important as the financial returns on their assets. Merrill Lynch promises financial advisers who become "an expert in you." If you want the boomers' money, these firms have concluded, you have to hold their hand through their transition to a new stage of life.

The gaping holes in many boomers' personal finances make it unsurprising that work is becoming the centerpiece of many ad campaigns. Just as insurance companies in the 1950s used the hook of leisure to make a virtue out of the necessity to move older workers out of the labor force, financial services companies are now seeking to use fulfillment and purpose to make a virtue out of the necessity of continued work.

Ameriprise pairs an older African American father and his grown son, who appears to be a leading-edge boomer. The message could apply to either one: "I've had three jobs already. And two kids going to college. I plan to work when I retire. But I won't have a job. I'll have a passion."

Paine Webber provides a compelling example with a photograph of a handsome young woman sitting with her aging boomer mother. "You're psyched about the future. You're full of new ideas. You're looking to start a business. *You're the one on the right.*" Referring to the older woman on the right, the message continues: "*They say* retirement means the end of your working years. *We say* plan well—so you can redefine retirement any time and any way you want. For many, it will be a bridge to a second career. A new business. Or a true labor of love."

Morgan Stanley presents a trim, stylish man—dark hair with graying temples—at a modern desk in a loft-like office setting. Intent, engaged, on the phone, laptop opened at the side, he offers this message to fellow boomers: "Retire? I'm not dead yet," he states, followed by the question: "Who made sixty the magical number? I want to stay in the game, for as long as I can. Maybe I'll start a company. Maybe I need someone to help me examine my options. After all, if I stayed home all day, my wife would probably divorce me."

Many of these appeals reveal something new struggling to break free of something old: In short, a next-generation vision of work constrained by a last-generation expectation of retirement. The result is an ungainly collection of oxymorons.

As Ellen Hoffman of *Business Week* writes: "On my desk is a pile of recent surveys and studies that purport to be about retirement. Yet when I open them up and actually read them, the main issue they seem to address is working—'in retirement.'"

Fortune promises advice on how to "Retire to the Job You Love," as *Kiplinger's* does in "Retire to Your Dream Job."

While *Smart Money* offers tips on "Retiring to Work," the *Philadelphia Inquirer* headlines, "After Retirement, A New Job." *U.S. News and World Report* asks incredulously, "You Call This Retirement?"

The retirement sections and retirement guides of magazines have become, by any measure, largely about work. The cover of *Smart Money*'s retirement issue, headlined "The New Retirement," features a time-lapse drawing of an aging boomer, white haired but fit as any thirty-year-old, rising out of his lounge chair into business suit and briefcase. The 2006 *U.S. News and World Report*'s "Annual Retirement Guide" went even further, making a comprehensive case against retirement with the cover headline, "7 Reasons Not to Retire—Why Continuing to Work Can Improve Your Health, Mental Sharpness—Even Your Marriage."

The oxymoronic phrase "retirement job" has become an ever-present part of the vocabulary. A Google search of the phrase yields nearly 50,000 links. The new employment site, RetirementJobs.com, features a section on "dream jobs" in retirement, among them BMW test driver, Christmas tree farmer, Feng Shui consultant, Zamboni driver, yoga instructor, and movie critic.

Even retirement communities are being designed increasingly around work. Del Webb, now part of Pulte Homes, in 1998 selected the distinctly un-sunny Chicago suburb of Huntley for the first northern Sun City location, a response to the growing desire of "active adults" not only for proximity to children and grandchildren, but to work. Many of the homes have offices built into them. "The boomers are healthy, they haven't saved a lot of money, they expect Social Security will run into problems," Steve A. Burch, national vice president for strategic marketing for Pulte told the *New York Times*. "So we want to let them live the Del Webb lifestyle and still work outside the home."

Perhaps the best commentary on all these strange juxta-positions is offered by Peter Drake, vice president for Fidelity Investments in Toronto. "The fact that so many boomers are planning to both retire early and then keep on working raises a very interesting question," Drake said. "If you work in retirement, are you actually retired?"

The answer is no. First we stretched retirement from a brief hiatus that was supposed to cover the few remaining years between disability and death and turned it into a period lasting fifteen, twenty, twenty-five years. It became grotesque, unworkable for individuals and unsustainable for American society. More recently, we've been stretching the meaning of the word until it becomes similarly meaningless.

A New Stage of Work

Peter Laslett got one thing wrong.

Believing that the great gift of an extra phase of life should be equally a benefit for third agers and for the broader society, Laslett envisioned individuals not only developing themselves but taking new responsibility for future generations. However, he saw this happening primarily through lifelong learning and volunteering, a view that made sense through his lens of the late 1980s.

This notion of freedom from work comes through in other thinkers as well. Zuboff's notion that the second half of life is about choice rather than compulsion is appealing, but in truth, this stage will be a combination of both choice and compulsion for most people. Many individuals feel compelled to work for financial or psychological or social reasons, or for all three, yet they want to choose how they work and what they work for. Instead of the liberation from labor entirely, they see an extra measure of freedom—in many cases to swap money for meaning, to do work that they couldn't afford to do earlier but can do now that children have grown and other ambitions have waned.

The financial services ad campaigns are a window on the popular psyche, and they indicate that the pull of work with passion and purpose is even more powerful than the promise of an upgrade to a better version of retirement. These marketers have not gone soft. Their campaigns were not produced by their charitable foundations, nor by their departments of corporate social responsibility. They are the result of focus groups and surveys of what their target audiences are looking for. And what they are looking for is the same thing Civic Ventures found in the 2005 New Face of Work study: They want work that is personally fulfilling, work that makes a difference in the world.

Fidelity was one of the first to tap this vein several years ago with a series of ads that showed aging boomers moving into teaching, swapping money for meaning and impact. One depicts a fifty-something man, brimming with engagement, in front of a science class, and offers a new definition of what matters: "See Yourself Succeeding," states the banner above the blackboard.

Another ad appears in transcript form, capturing a conversation between Fidelity investor and Fidelity representative.

Investor: I'm looking to shake things up a bit.

Fidelity Rep: With your investments?

Investor: With my life, I've been working for twenty-five years. Now I want to do what I want, not what I feel I should.

Fidelity Rep: Wow. Good for you. What is it you're looking for?

Investor: I've always wanted to be a teacher. But it doesn't pay as well as I'm used to . . . so I need to be prepared.

Fidelity Rep: Yes, I understand. We should probably start by looking at your current portfolio. Then we can help you create an investment and income strategy that may help boost your earnings.

Investor: That's what I was hoping . . .

Fidelity Rep: We'll get you in front of those kids while still trying to maintain your lifestyle.

Investor: That's good. I mean, I'd like to give something back.

Lincoln Financial Group has likewise sponsored an extensive campaign focused directly on the freedom to work in ways that promote individual and social renewal. One ad shows a door that reads "Guidance Counselor." The occupant, an attractive white-haired African American woman, sits talking with a promising high school student. The message: "There are ways to leave a legacy without having a wing of a building named after you." Another ad advises: "Do something big while there's still time to put it in your autobiography."

One series of ads from Lincoln has been running so long we've seen the woman, identified on Lincoln's Web site as "Gloria," evolve in her new career. She's sixty-one, "been busy with clinical work in Manhattan for twenty-seven years" and is ready to end her private practice. She's "newly single," "relishing life," and "certainly isn't ready to 'retire' just yet" in any overall sense. Looking a bit like Meryl Streep with a stethoscope around her neck, Gloria holds a child somewhere in Africa, echoing the work of Doctors Without Borders.

Laslett, who called for those in the third age to create

their own new paths and institutions, might well approve of this peculiarly American way of constructing the new stage. Progress in the United Kingdom, he said, had been "encouraging but slight." He was counting on America not only to develop a more robust vision of this stage of life but to fashion a new set of institutions to realize its possibilities.

"The emergence of the Third Age in the United States and the adoption of a fresh map of life will," he wrote, "be one of the most important of all social developments at the turn of the twentieth to the twenty-first century."

Ed Speedling

*Health Care Executive
to Advocate for the Homeless*

The high school I went to was the Catholic high school that took you if no other Catholic high school would take you. It was the bottom of the barrel, and you knew it. It was like a step up from a reform school. I wanted nothing to do with school. The happiest day of my life was when I finally got out of high school. I leaped off of the steps. I was a free man.

And then I went to night school at Fordham University's business school. When I got there, it was like, "Wow!" The teachers were respectful, people were adults, and, my God, it was kind of nice. I got very interested in economics and organizations and health care.

In the early 1970s, I landed a position in the Nursing Department at the Mt. Sinai Medical Center in upper Manhattan, where I started a new division of clinical evaluation. I was promoted to assistant director of the department and was invited to join the faculty of the Medical School as an instructor in community medicine. There, I conducted research and taught freshman medical students the connections between illness and family dynamics.

I was very ambitious in those days. Why was I driven? Who knows? I grew up in a working-class neighborhood where everyone was struggling. You just saw the unhappiness, the fights, the violence. It was a real struggle. I guess when I began to move into a different place, I wanted to get far away from that world.

Still, I couldn't shake the memory of something that happened in 1961, on my way to night classes at the City University of New York. I came out of the subway station onto a street in upper Manhattan and was confronted by a middle-aged woman in a long, shabby gray coat. She told me she needed some money because she was hungry. Now growing up in New York City, one gets used to seeing people in all circumstances. But I was moved by this woman, perhaps because she was so close to me and her plea was aimed specifically at me, no one else was around. I took a dollar out of my pocket, gave it to her, and hurried off to my class. The following Sunday, the encounter still fresh in my mind, I asked a priest I knew whether I should have done more to help the woman. He said no, not to worry, that my response to her was adequate. I walked away unconvinced.

The years between 1961 and 1999 were rich ones—Ph.D.,

publications, promotions, and interesting work in outstanding medical schools and university hospitals. I am grateful for all of it. However, as the years wore on, I became increasingly aware of a yearning, at first vague but later unmistakable, to move to a place where I could work with people who, like the woman at the subway station, lived on the edge of desperation.

Finally, in my late fifties—awareness of the passing years was a definite factor for me—I decided that I had to do something. With tremendous support from my wife, I embarked on a serious assessment of what I was really after. I read and reflected, talked for hours with people who cared about me, and waited in silence to discern a direction.

Part of this process was about me: Did I really want to radically change my lifestyle, leave a career that had been good to me for over twenty-five years? Were there other options, like moving to part-time work (which I discussed with my superiors, and actually tried to implement)? What was really motivating me—was I running away or moving forward?

The process had to include my family and my responsibilities to wife and children. Three children still lived at home; one had just graduated from college. How would they be affected emotionally? I had reason to be concerned. When I brought the subject up, I heard reactions from the kids like: "Does this mean we will be poor?" "Can I still go to college?" "Are you okay, Dad?" Money was a consideration. How much would I need to make to take care of the things that the family needed? How would this affect my wife, a college professor who was herself contemplating a career change? Then there was the question: What would I actually do?

Once the decision to change careers was made, I had to face the prospect of actually looking for a job. It had been a long time since I was on the job market, much less in a field that I had almost no familiarity with. But I was optimistic. After all, I had a great résumé—several pages detailing my competencies and accomplishments. The real problem, I thought, would be how to choose from the many offers I would receive from eager executive directors grateful for having the chance to hire someone like me.

Well, it didn't turn out the way I expected. I did manage to get in to see a number of senior officials in a variety of non-profit organizations. This resulted in some very interesting conversations but no job offers. Looking back, I realize that I didn't know the field of social service nearly as much as I needed to. I couldn't articulate clearly enough what I was looking for. I know I didn't want to be an executive director, program manager, or head of an evaluation unit, which were the kinds of positions I was most often asked about in interviews.

Moreover, I couldn't move beyond saying things like, "I want to help people," or "I want to give back." And when I did manage to say that I just wanted to work in the trenches, the interview moved to the end phase. It went on like this until my wife remembered that she had taught someone who went into social work from a lucrative career in business. He was now employed in a leadership position in a Philadelphia organization that worked with vulnerable people, including those who had become homeless. Maybe he could help.

It didn't take long for him to grasp what I was looking for. He had been there himself. He wrote out the telephone number of Reverend Kevin Lawrence, the director of St. John's Hospice. He was looking for someone to supervise the social services program at the shelter. "But I don't want a big position" I said. "Ed," he replied, "this is a homeless shelter. There will be no secretary, maybe an office, maybe not. And definitely no expense account. Call him!"

When I walked into St. John's, it was love at first sight. It was really the fulfillment of a deep desire to work with the poor, to align myself with people who are vulnerable—not a policymaking position but a personal involvement. That's what was driving me, and that was what I gained tremendously there.

A few years later, in order to get a different perspective on homelessness, I took a position at Project H.O.M.E., another outstanding organization that offers a broad range of services to both address homelessness and prevent it.

Homelessness is so complex. The more you get into it, the more complex it is. You listen to the men and women talk about their lives and you see the impact of families that don't work, neighborhoods that are battlegrounds, kids who have no childhood, the sexual abuse of children, both boys and girls, the other kinds of abuse. It's unbelievable what we allow to happen to our children and particularly to our poor children, and I think that's where it all starts.

There's this one homeless guy I have lunch with sometimes, and he really struggles with alcohol. We talk about understanding the different ways that people try to help him. He just convinces me of the importance of not trying to solve his problem, but just sitting down and having lunch with him because I value him, and I'm getting as much out of the conversation as he is, maybe more. It's a profoundly simple but very elusive understanding—that you reach people by being their equal and not by being their teacher, their counselor, their whatever. You have to be their equal and be able to see them on their terms and be able to have a give-and-take.

Lately, I'm more and more pulled into things like strategic planning work. This is beginning to look like my previous work. I'm being pulled away from being out on the streets and really working at that level, you know. It's a dilemma, because how can I say no to that? This is what the organization really needs me to do. The challenge for the organization is to take advantage of the competencies that I bring, without pigeonholing me. I have regular "out-of-role" experiences at my organization, and I enjoy spending some time in the conference room with senior administrators. I know I have something of value to bring to the table. It feels good to help, but it also feels good when I return to the trenches.

I'm working on drawing some boundaries so that I'm able to find time to be out in the street, time to be with family, time to think on my own. It is a tough balancing act, and I have considered quitting. When I left my last position in health care, I worried about how to leave in a way that left the department I headed intact and most of my colleagues unaffected. But when I think about leaving my current job, my conscience asks, how can I leave? It's a great organization, with a great mission.

Working here is so dynamic; it's so alive. We have many great young people. It's a wonderful way for me to feel I'm part of something that's happening, that I'm not just chewing over the past. I'm seeing in these young people what the world can be like. It's very hopeful.

CHAPTER FIVE

Contested Terrain

A greeter greets people," says Jim Churchman, sixty-six, a greeter at a Wal-Mart store in Columbia, Missouri. "I try to project that there's a happy spot in life, that everybody can find some happiness each day. If you come to Wal-Mart, you usually come to buy something, but if you don't, that's fine. I'm spreading goodwill."

Churchman tells his story in the book *Gig*, which recounts the experience of working in America. Churchman, who has a master's degree and a doctorate in education, worked as a schoolteacher and principal in Illinois and Missouri for forty years. "Those were good years for me," he says. "I was happy most always." He particularly liked fifth- and sixth-graders, because they are "still pretty nice and don't know everything yet."

When he first retired, he played a lot of golf. "I got tired of that pretty quick," he says. "I didn't feel like I had much self-worth . . . I just didn't really like being retired . . . I didn't know what to do with myself all day. I got bored. I felt lazy." Eating lunch at the nearby McDonald's one day, he saw Wal-Mart workers unloading freight. "I thought, 'That's what I need.' So I asked for a job."

Churchman's first job at Wal-Mart was on the loading docks. His people skills helped him win the lighter-duty job of greeter, welcoming and directing customers near the front door for forty hours a week.

He cut back his hours when his wife got cancer, working only until noon or one o'clock. "I'll probably stay here as long as they have a need for me," he says. After five years at Wal-Mart, he is quick to say, "I don't think there should be a set age for retirement. I've got years to go before I want to quit working here. I like it and it keeps me busy."

Such part-time "bridge" jobs in retail and other sectors have become a popular route for those seeking a paid job after the end of a first career phase, to ease the way toward the presumed goal, full retirement. Joseph Quinn, professor of economics at Boston College, estimates that as many as one-third to one-half of older Americans hold some kind of bridge job before retiring completely. Retirement, he observes, has become "a process, not a single event."

Bridge jobs fill real needs, for both employers and employees. Such jobs add a fourth leg—earned income—to the increasingly rickety three-legged stool of pensions, savings, and Social Security that once secured personal finances after primary careers ended. Beyond pay and benefits, the appeal for many is work itself—the social connections, the daily routines, the chance to help people.

And such jobs demonstrate the increasing value of a long-undervalued segment of the worker population to retailers and other employers that face growing labor shortages. Some employers, to be sure, are simply looking for individuals desperate for a job that pays rock-bottom wages without health coverage or other benefits. But an increasing number of employers see the value of responsible, stable grown-ups who know what's expected in the workplace and have a track record of experience.

Home Depot, for example, has teamed with AARP to recruit plumbers, electricians, landscapers, designers, sales associates, and customer service representatives, with an ad campaign built on the theme "Passion Never Retires."

For men (and some women) whose passion has shifted from their day job to their tool shed, Home Depot promises to make their hobby center stage—and throw in a paycheck as well. (There is the added advantage of the opportunity to provide advice, wanted and otherwise, to dozens of customers each day.) Home Depot offers part-timers health and other benefits, including tuition reimbursement and discounted stock-purchase plans, as well as flexibility about schedules and locations that lets workers move between stores, allowing them, for example, to fly south for the winter months.

Building on the Home Depot campaign, AARP has

recruited thirty companies to its "national employer team," including Walgreen's, Borders, Principal Financial, Pitney Bowes, and Verizon, as well as "temp" services such as Adecco and Kelly Services.

In his book *50+*, AARP CEO Bill Novelli describes how Borders, the giant book chain, implemented a formal policy to increase the ranks of workers over fifty from 6 percent in the late 1990s to 16 percent today—with a goal of 25 percent by 2010. With people over forty-five purchasing half of all books sold in the United States, Borders found a solid business case for hiring workers in the same age category.

Borders also discovered that workers over fifty were easier to recruit and train, as well as being smart, energetic, and dependable—and had a turnover rate one-tenth that of workers younger than thirty. Borders now considers older workers so valuable that, like Home Depot, it recently added medical and dental benefits for part-time workers, tailoring the package to this population by including a vision plan, prescription drug coverage, a disability payment, and a long-term care option. Borders also offers a "corporate passport" that gives workers the flexibility to move between store locations.

Benefits and flexibility—in hours and locations—is increasingly important to boomers, many of whom are still raising their own kids while caring for aging parents. Study after study has shown that workers over the age of fifty prize the ability to break free of the lockstep work schedule that characterizes so many jobs. A survey of workers age fifty-four to seventy-four found that nearly half wanted to work significantly fewer hours, but neither the pay and benefits nor the jobs themselves were organized to allow them to do so.

For older women who leave the workforce, nearly one-fourth report they did so to take care of an aged parent, a grandchild, or another family member. "For a large percentage of those workers, flexibility would provide the answer to extending their careers while also allowing them to attend their many demands outside of work," reports the Alfred P. Sloan Foundation, a leader in workforce development issues.

For all the merits of the best of the bridge jobs, it is essential that this category not become the only option, the standard expectation, or the default position for individuals working in the second half of life. Splitting the difference between work and leisure, midlife careers and traditional retirement, the old expectation and new possibilities, bridge jobs deliver a form of semiretirement characterized by gradual disengagement and downward mobility. That beats falling off (or being pushed over) an arbitrary cliff at sixty, but all too often it amounts to a sliding board heading in pretty much the same direction.

Indeed, as lives come full circle, the subtle implication is that so too should careers, with jobs at the end resembling the low-paid, part-time, retail, or, at best, semi-entrepreneurial, jobs of our youth—though perhaps with "greeting" replacing lawn mowing.

Most important, bridge jobs fall far short of a powerful vision of purpose or contribution to accompany the historic emergence of a new stage of life and work. They are not up to the task of recapturing in any significant way one of the greatest investments in this nation's history: the education, training, and health of the baby boom generation.

"Most jobs are mismatched with the competencies, needs and preferences of older workers," concluded a Sloan Foundation report. The foundation documented that many people who want to continue working in their fifties, sixties, and seventies find they have few choices beyond continuing at the same job on a full-time basis or seeking part-time, bridge job—like work, often at low wages with few benefits. Boston College's Quinn, a leading expert on the phenomenon, finds that "[b]ridge jobs generally represent a movement down the socioeconomic ladder, from white collar to blue collar, or from skilled to less skilled."

Are the Wal-Mart Years poised to replace the Golden Years as the new norm for the second half of life? That outcome is far from assured. Compelling alternatives are beginning to take shape for individuals searching for more in their next ten or twenty years at work. Indeed, work in the second half of life is becoming increasingly contested terrain.

At stake is one of the largest potential transformation of work in America in half a century, since millions of women moved into the labor market with different ideas about what it means to work—in other words, since the last time everything changed.

A Higher Calling

Retailers offering bridge jobs may be the most aggressive recruiters of men and women over fifty entering a new stage of work, but they're not the only ones. Another "industry" is innovating to seize this population as a way to alleviate talent shortages: the Catholic Church.

In Hales Corners, Wisconsin, the men at the Sacred Heart School of Theology are looking for work that is very different from a bridge job. As "second career" seminarians, they are making one of the most significant commitments an individual can make in the world today. The seminary is asking for the deepest commitment of soul and spirit, looking for men prepared to turn their lives over to a higher purpose. Such a job is truly a vocation, coming from the Latin *vocare*, "to call." The school represents anything but splitting the difference.

The average age of seminarians is in the mid-forties, though many are in their fifties and sixties. Four out of five have decided to train for the Catholic priesthood after completing their first careers.

Men who have decided to become priests after the death of their wives make up nearly one-fifth of Sacred Heart's students. "I'm sure you have probably heard people say, 'How does a priest know how I feel?'" says one seminarian, Mike McLain, a widower in his mid-fifties. He and the other widowers "will know how they feel," continues McLain, "because we've been there and I think that's going to be an important part of our ministry."

The priests of the Sacred Heart are known as SCJs, for Sacré-Coeur de Jésus, the order's French name. According to *The Collar*, Jonathan Englert's study of the Hales Corners seminary, Sacred Heart purchased the land for the seminary from a group of Dominican sisters in 1929. The former convent was for decades the order's American headquarters as well as a seminary. As interest in the priesthood surged in the 1960s, SCJ leaders decided to expand and modernize the Sacred Heart School, adding dorms and chapels, classrooms and sports fields, dining halls and administrative facilities.

Then the priesthood labor market collapsed. In 1965, there were 8,325 graduate-level seminarians in America. By 2003, the number had plummeted to 3,414, even as the U.S. Catholic population increased by nearly 50 percent, from 45 million in the 1960s to almost 65 million today.

At Sacred Heart, Englert writes, the new facility that was designed to accommodate hundreds of seminarians and faculty could count just forty students by the early 1970s—and a balloon payment on the buildings was looming. The order was barely able to make the loan payment and was sagging under the ongoing costs of maintaining a massively underused facility.

The Sacred Heart leadership decided to make a virtue out of this crisis. When the flow of young seminarians had been strong, the Catholic Church had seen no need for men older than forty, who were deemed to be less well suited to religious life and promised fewer years of service. Now, Sacred Heart moved aggressively to recruit "older men with delayed, or second-career, vocations," according to Englert. Such adaptability was part of the order's history. In nineteenth-century Germany, mandatory military service had prevented younger men from entering the seminary. "The SCJs had embraced older seminarians," Englert writes. "They knew the process worked."

Sacred Heart established its Center for Adult Religious Vocations. Attending the school is more like going to a military academy than a graduate school and requires sponsorship before the student can even apply. Students come from all over the country. According to Father Tom Knoebel, who has been at Sacred Heart since 1981, older candidates come because they feel a need to be of service to others and think their secular lives will have great value in the priesthood, as they bring more skills with them than a young man in his teens or early twenties. Nearly half of all incoming students have a master's or doctorate in some other field.

An older candidate "makes a more mature, thoughtful decision to enter the ministry," Knoebel says. "He is used to the ups and downs and challenges of life, so he is not as discouraged when confronted with a problem."

Simple supply and demand is driving the focus on second-career individuals. "The Catholic priest shortage is severe, so any concern over ordaining older men is kind of stupid," Knoebel comments. "The concern is based on a false model of careers, where you start at something in your 20s and stay with it until death. Those days are over. Let's encourage young people to enter the priesthood, sure, but it is foolish to turn your back on someone who can offer you 10 or 20 years of high quality service."

Sacred Heart's retention rates are significantly higher than those of traditional seminaries. Overall, 12–15 percent of young men ordained as Catholic priests have left the ministry. For the second-career priests at Sacred Heart, just 5–6 percent of graduates since the late 1970s have left active ministry, excluding those who retired or died.

Other Catholic institutions are also seeking out older recruits. Labor shortages in the priesthood have driven The Pope John XXIII National Seminary in Weston, Massachusetts, a Jesuit school, to focus on training second-career priests. And Catholic churches around the country have been actively recruiting individuals in the second half of life for lay ecclesial ministers and deacons, two non-clergy positions.

Lay ecclesial ministers are typically paid parish staffers or volunteers who work closely with priests in particular areas of ministry, helping to free priests to perform those duties exclusively theirs. Frequently these lay positions require a master's degree. Ordained deacons, who can be married, have been able since 1968 to perform baptisms, officiate at marriages, and provide communion. Their focus is frequently on service to the community. As the recruitment Web site vocations.com explains, "The deacon reaches out to the poor, the sick, the elderly, the divorced, the imprisoned and others in order to first address their human needs."

Growth in the number of second-career individuals entering these fields has been dramatic. A staggering 95 percent of all diaconate candidates in the United States today are over the age of forty, 63 percent are over fifty, and almost all are married men, according to a 2006 study by the Center for Applied Research in the Apostolate at Georgetown University. In lay ecclesial ministry programs, 75 percent of candidates are over forty and 44 percent are over fifty; most are women.

"Our students are in their 40s, and they have been wondering, 'Is that all there is?'" Knoebel states. "Money and sex and power are just not doing it for them and they feel there must be more to life. They are seeing deeper meanings that have more to do with generosity, being of service, and contributing to the betterment of others."

The New Hybrid

Ed Speedling launched his encore career to focus on the same priorities as the men who arrive at Sacred Heart— deeper meaning, generosity, the chance to be of service and contribute to the betterment of others. And he even ended up working at two organizations with links to the Catholic Church—St. John's Hospice in Philadelphia, and then Project H.O.M.E., led by Sister Mary Scullion.

Nevertheless, Speedling's search for a calling demonstrates that the quest for more meaning at work the second time around does not require entering a seminary, just as the need for continued income need not lead inexorably to working at Wal-Mart. An encore career focused on social change is an appealing response to the call to more meaningful work, one blending the spirit of social impact with the pragmatic need for real pay and benefits.

This route is a departure from the traditional expectation of how people are supposed to channel the impulse toward doing good in the second half of life.

If Speedling had been born a generation earlier, any instinct to make a difference at this juncture might have taken him on a fairly predictable path, perhaps pitching in over the holidays or volunteering at a homeless shelter as an adjunct to retirement. Historically, those in their fifties or sixties or older who decided they wanted to heal the world, to tend to its problems, to do some good for others have long been steered toward "senior volunteerism," where their impulses may or may not be deployed in ways that have a real impact.

From the outset, Speedling focused on finding a paying job with the potential to add significantly to his life's work. For one thing, he needed the income. A successful professional, he had held a series of management positions spanning several decades. But he was by no means wealthy, in a position to live primarily on his savings for an extended period lasting decades in duration. He still had family responsibilities, including college tuition for his children, to worry about.

Speedling was likewise intent on working with homeless people in a way that not only ameliorated suffering but addressed the root causes of homelessness. He was not looking to do charity work or to work superficially on tough issues. Any chance at genuine impact in a new field would require his full energy, focus, and commitment.

Indeed, tackling homelessness, school reform, climate change, economic development, health care, and other major challenges of our time requires more than pitching in on the margins. As Robert Egger, founder of the D.C. Central Kitchen and author of *Begging for Change*, says, we cannot "charity away problems like homelessness, poverty, abuse and exclusion." Egger decries "the folly of trying to fix big . . . problems using our 'extra, left over' stuff like spare time, end of the year money, surplus food or used clothing."

Just as traditional "senior volunteering" cannot fully satisfy the impulse to contribute in significant ways, most available work options in the second half of life cannot fully satisfy the impulse to work that is significant and deeply satisfying. A significant gap persists. There is no real category or way to think about this stage of work, and there are few established avenues for talented and motivated people like Speedling, who want to fashion a powerful and coherent body of work out of their passion for solving problems and making the world better.

Encore careers hold the potential to fill that gap, offering work with powerful psychological and spiritual meaning that contributes to the well-being of others and draws on the true gifts and experience of the individual. They simultaneously provide a practical answer to the challenges of financing a new stage of life that may extend for twenty or thirty years or more.

Despite these many virtues (and some promising inroads), the social sector, unlike retailers or even the Catholic Church, has not yet mounted a concerted effort to recruit aging boomers into encore careers. Most organizations in the arena remain handicapped by old attitudes and arrangements. And that has left it to a new generation of individuals to plow their own paths to purpose and passion. As these people assemble their hybrid careers—finding real jobs that also let them find their calling—they are creating alternatives to the bridge job and other models that otherwise could become the default option for the new stage of work.

Dave Miller is one example. He didn't know what he was going to do when he left BellSouth after a thirty-year career in marketing, sales, regulatory affairs, public relations, and customer service. But for at least five years before he left, an inner voice had been telling him, *You don't belong here anymore.* To which he says he tried to respond, *Well, sure I do.* A few months later, he'd hear it whispering again, *You just don't belong here anymore.*

It was his son, a high school graduate, who got Miller to listen. As his thirty-year anniversary at BellSouth approached, the younger Miller told him he wanted to go to Los Angeles to break into the music business. Miller had wanted him to go to college. "Dad," his son told him, "if I never go, I'm afraid I'm always gonna ask that question, 'What would have happened if . . . ?'"

That made Miller ask himself the same question. "'If I don't make this move, I'll always wonder fifteen years from now or ten years out, I'll wonder what my life would have been.' And I wondered if I would regret it."

He gave himself six to eight months to "just kind of do nothing," decompress, and take a month-long vacation out west. Back in Charlotte, North Carolina, he started making calls, working his network, asking people, "What could a person with the skills that I think I have do, you know, where would I fit in?" Then he met with the founder of Crisis Assistance Ministry, which provides about 70,000 people each year with clothing, appliances, and financial assistance, to keep them from becoming homeless. The head of the clothing and furniture program had just left.

Miller was hired and over time asked for more responsibilities. Now sixty-four, he is director of operations, responsible for all parts of the program.

Leslie Hawke also began tentatively, with a nagging sense that something was missing in her life—and the willingness to take a step at a time. After decades as a middle manager, mostly in large corporations, Hawke was taking the subway to her work at an Internet company in New York City. "It stopped at 59th Street, and I remember distinctly looking out on the platform at Columbus Circle from inside of an over-packed subway car and thinking, *If you died tomorrow, you would be so embarrassed at how you have been spending your life.*

When she got to her office, she looked up the Peace Corps on the Web. Six months later, she was in Romania, helping a community development program in Bacau, a city in the northeastern part of the country. When her assignment ended, she stayed. Her experience with a young boy who was begging near her apartment led her to start a nonprofit called Gata, Dispus si Capabil (Ready, Willing and Able), helping children to get an education and working with mothers to increase their income and with neighborhoods to improve living conditions.

For her fifty- to sixty-hour workweeks, Hawke gets a salary of about $18,000 a year, plus $500 in living expenses, "a lot less than I would need in order to live in the U.S. at a comparable level of comfort." But her financial fears have faded as her sense of purpose has blossomed. "When I was contemplating entering the Peace Corps, if I had seriously thought I might wind up in Romania for the rest of my life I would have been scared to death. But now that's just what I hope happens!"

Frederick A.O. "Fritz" Schwarz knew exactly what he wanted to do when he completed his midlife career: the same high-powered legal work he had done his entire professional life. But he wanted cases that focused on the public interest, shifting from the mostly private sector clients he represented as a top partner at Cravath, Swaine & Moore, one of the nation's most elite law firms. It also marked a return to the periodic stints in public service that had punctuated Schwarz's private legal career—and to his earlier days as an idealistic law student who organized picketing of a Woolworth store in Cambridge, Massachusetts, to support sit-ins by blacks in the South.

As he approached his sixties, he was already engaged in contemplating and preparing for this new chapter. Finishing up his cases and finding the right situation to make the transition took a number of years, but Schwarz then went to work as senior counsel at the nonprofit Brennan Center for Justice at NYU Law School. His work at the Brennan Center is aimed at advancing campaign finance reform, voting rights, and civil liberties, and he even stepped in to serve as interim director for the Center when the organization went through a leadership change.

Looking back at his previous work, Schwarz notes that writing a compelling brief for one of Cravath's corporate clients provided much the same intellectual stimulation as his current efforts on behalf of those represented by the Brennan Center: "But in another sense you're working for public interest instead of working for money—and working for public interest gives you a satisfaction that working for money doesn't."

The payoff is hardly restricted to the benefits felt by Schwarz himself. In crafting a new role for Schwarz, the Brennan Center gained the services of one of the most talented legal practitioners in the country. When *American Lawyer* magazine announced its first lifetime achievement awards in 2004, on the occasion of the magazine's twenty-fifth anniversary, Schwarz was among the ten individuals honored. According to *American Lawyer*, "Schwarz retired from private practice last year—not to the driving range or the fishing boat," but to a new stage of work dedicated to "issues at the heart of American democracy."

The paths that Speedling, Miller, Hawke, and Schwarz are carving out for themselves are in many ways distinct—and there is little realization among them of being part of something larger. They don't even have a language to describe what they are undertaking. The early innovators constructing encore careers have done so largely on their own, by hook and by crook, by adapting the available resources to their own needs and by themselves being adaptable to opportunities and surprises. They are cobbling together a wide array of strategies for finding work that blends the goals of doing well and doing good.

As the accumulated experience of these individuals begins to reach critical mass, it is possible to discern patterns and insights that both help to define the emerging shape of this new phase of work and provide some guidance to those contemplating their own encore career.

A BODY OF WORK. The encore career is not a retirement job. It's not a transitional phase. It's not a bridge between the end of real work and the beginning of real leisure. It's not leftover time to be killed. It's an entire stage of life and work—a destination and a category of work unto itself.

The extended time horizon fundamentally changes conventional thinking about career arcs. Those retooling for a decade or longer can justify going back to school, getting training, or moving to a new location. They can allow themselves time to make a few mistakes before finding the right fit. They can even pursue a *second* encore career or, eventually, true retirement.

It's also worth remembering that an encore career is more than a job—it could comprise a collection of jobs and other engagements that have a weight and coherence taken together, a true body of work.

PRACTICAL IDEALISM. Encore careers blend clear-eyed pragmatism and the determination to make a better world, the idealism of a generation tempered by years of experience at making things work.

Much of this work will take place in the nonprofit and public sector—but the private sector also provides an appealing route. Indeed, *Motto*, the new magazine created by two former *Wall Street Journal* reporters, is targeting those pursuing a new model of work at the intersection of "passion, purpose, and profits."

For most boomers who want to make a deep commitment to this new amalgam, drawing a salary will be an important part of the encore equation. Some will be able to take a salary that's a fraction of their value on the open market, even in the nonprofit world. For others, like members of Experience Corps, even a small monthly stipend makes a sustained and deep commitment financially feasible.

Even for those who have minimal financial need, income cements the contract. Whether we like it or not, paid work is likely to be taken more seriously by both workers and employers.

AN EXTRA MEASURE OF FREEDOM. If notions such as phased retirement and the bridge job split the difference between work and leisure, the encore career stands for a different formulation—a combination of the commitment to productivity and contribution associated with work, and the freedom to choose how we spend our time associated with retirement.

This is an essential point for financial planning and social policy: With retirement no longer the central goal for what's next, the objective of financial planning is no longer the ability to forgo income altogether. Planning and saving is still important, but the objective changes: to saving enough to buy *choice* in and about work, to wrest the extra measure of freedom that allows work with passion and purpose in service of a better world. That often and appropriately also means the potential for greater flexibility in work.

Sometimes a buyout, a pension, or even an involuntary layoff provides the extra measure of freedom, and the impetus, to embark on something new. Compensation from an encore career may not, by itself, match the income level of a primary career. But combining a pension, a Social Security check, or a severance package with even modest compensation may make it possible to pursue passion and purpose rather than pay.

JUMPING THE GUN. Lives are getting longer, while careers are getting shorter. Indeed, the longevity revolution is only part of the reason a new stage of life is being shaped. The other reason is that so many are finishing their first career earlier.

In this context, it pays to be proactive: beginning with an assumption from the outset of the likelihood of a second career (or two or three). That means planning financially for this eventuality, but also developing a parallel career, providing the platform for a later encore phase. Fritz Schwarz urges young lawyers who think they might want a public service phase of their work to "cast their bread upon the waters," to begin through pro bono work and networking and other opportunities to build the experience and ties that will later enable that transition.

Most encore pioneers are not waiting until sixty-five to launch this new phase, submitting earlier to that voice that says that one career has run its course and it is time to look for something different and more meaningful. And making the transition early means more time and less stress in navigating the transition.

REALISM NOT REINVENTION. The romance of reinvention is part of the American character. But this fantasy is a hazard for those setting out on their next chapter. The fact is, we remain the people we were, even as the trappings change. More appropriate to the new stage of work is the language of renewal, a rekindling of passion and the prospect of ongoing learning, growth, and challenge.

Realistic expectations of the challenges of working in education or health care, or becoming a social or business entrepreneur, are key. In the real world of the social sector, confusion and ambiguity exist along with bright shining moments. Most employers are not yet sophisticated about how to make efficient and intelligent use of the encore career talent pool.

Several years ago, *Fortune* did a story on retired business professionals attempting to move to the nonprofit sector, mostly through volunteer roles. The piece, "Candy Striper, My Ass!" chronicled their frustration, as they were shunted into roles that made a mockery of their accumulated experience and professional know-how.

It's not all age discrimination, even if the effect is the same. When Velma Simpson arrived at HUD, for example, her supervisors assumed she was simply passing through, and treated her accordingly. After all, everyone else at the agency in their fifties had one foot out the door. But Simpson was on an entirely different trajectory—ramping up rather than moving out. That pattern was unfamiliar in the organization.

For all these reasons, the experience of the encore pioneers underscores the necessity of ranging past marketing materials trumpeting the lofty goals and noble purpose of potential encore career employers to crafting internships and other opportunities that open onto the real, day-to-day experience of working for a particular group and provide a vehicle for trying on potential roles.

THE PERSISTENCE OF TRADE-OFFS. Most individuals describe their encore careers as a complex phenomenon, bringing together anticipated rewards and many, often unanticipated, challenges.

Ruth Van Demark, a Lutheran minister in the Wicker Park neighborhood of Chicago, didn't go to divinity school to become a construction manager. But shortly after arriving in her new role, reality intervened. Her church was either going to be fixed or condemned. So the building, the financing, and other business aspects of running Wicker Park Lutheran Church took at least as much time as pastoral counseling, delivering sermons, and mobilizing her congregation to promote social justice.

Encore careers often require trade-offs in family relationships, as one partner finds passion in a new pursuit waxing, while the other is losing interest in a career phase. Perhaps most powerful of all is the tension that many feel between a desire for flexibility and one for impact. Some positions can blend these desires, but in other roles, choosing one means sacrificing the other. Ed Speedling readily admits, for example, that it would be a challenge to do his job well or have nearly the impact he desires on a part-time basis. Yet he yearns for greater flexibility than he had in earlier career phases.

CONNECTIONS MATTER. Purpose and impact may motivate individuals to move into encore careers, but relations and connections often become just as important.

The individuals surveyed for the New Face of Work study confirmed that *people* are just as important as *purpose*. "Purposeful relationships" that are built around work and collective accomplishments that matter transcend the purely social connections we think of as a staple of retirement.

Some of the most important of these relationships span the generations. The art of mentoring is what lubricates the new multigenerational workplace, and it is an important driving force in the encore career experience. Many find the mentoring of younger professionals one of the most satisfying aspects of this new phase of work. The connection with these individuals is a kind of link with the future, promising an impact that will extend well beyond the end of the encore career.

INVENTING INSIDE AND OUT. Those not satisfied with available opportunities can often create their own.

Encore career innovators are contributing to the dramatic increase in the number of social ventures—nonprofit organizations or for-profit businesses with a social mission. In fact, over the past decade, adults aged fifty-five to sixty-four have been the group most likely to start new businesses, according to a study by the Ewing Marion Kauffman Foundation.

However, many are also trying to carve out new roles in existing organizations, often serving as change makers within those entities. There is much to be said for this strategy. While the nonprofit sector is in much need of innovation, and starting new organizations can help create new solutions and prod existing organizations, the hard work of transforming existing organizations from the inside is also essential.

One illustration is Mike Mulqueen, a retired Marine Corps general, who took over the food depository in Chicago. Mulqueen hired fellow "retirees" from NASA and Arthur Anderson, bringing a new efficiency to the organization and transforming it into one of the most successful food banks in the country.

AN EMERGING PATTERN. Those now preparing to launch their own encore careers may not be the first over the wall, but they remain pioneers. That means all the excitement of being on the vanguard of something new and big—along with all the obstacles and barriers. There is one major compensation: Those on the leading edge are not alone. Whether they realize it or not, they are part of something larger. On the surface, the seemingly disparate strands—those going back to school in such areas as education and divinity, joining the Peace Corps and Experience Corps, the new crops of second-half social entrepreneurs, those shifting from private sector careers to nonprofits, individuals moving from the military to a second round of service in the social sector or schools—are all part of the same emerging pattern, the encore career impulse.

Managing Oneself

The challenges of the encore career pioneers are not trivial, but they are central to what the late Peter Drucker, the greatest management theorist of the twentieth century, considered the signal development of our time.

When the history of our time is written in a few hundred years, Drucker wrote as he neared his own tenth decade, the most important feature will not be the Internet, technology, or medical science, but rather "an unprecedented change in the human condition." For the first time, Drucker said, "substantial and rapidly growing numbers of people have choices. For the first time, they will have to manage themselves."

"Most of us, even those with modest endowments," Drucker wrote in 1999, "will have to learn to develop ourselves. We will have to place ourselves where we can make the greatest contribution. And we will have to stay mentally alert and engaged during a 50-year working life, which will mean knowing how and when to change the work we do."

Drucker was a seminal thinker on organization, the author of more than thirty books on management and other topics. His 2004 essay, "What Makes an Effective Executive," shared the *Harvard Business Review*'s annual award for most significant article of the year (among the traits: "focus on opportunities rather than problems"), the seventh time Drucker had received the honor. When he died the next year at ninety-five, *Business Week*'s cover story called him "The Man Who Invented Management."

Given today's lifespans, Drucker believed that self-management is more critical today than ever before. In the past, he observed, if you were fortunate enough to survive forty years working on the railroad or in a factory, "You were quite happy to spend the rest of your life doing nothing." But that has all changed.

Today, knowledge workers in particular "are not 'finished' after 40 years on the job, they are merely bored." To Drucker, the talk about midlife crisis for the professional worker is mostly about boredom. He wrote that most individuals, by age forty-five, are good at their jobs, "but they are not learning or contributing or deriving challenge and satisfaction from the job." Nonetheless, they face another two, three, or even four decades of work.

"That is why managing oneself increasingly leads one to begin a second career," Drucker wrote. Drucker acknowledged there are many pathways to such encores, and that second careers themselves would have different shapes, depending on whether they were jobs in established organizations, new start-ups, or moonlighting interests that turn into full-time jobs.

In particular, Drucker predicted a surge of interest in non-profit work and social entrepreneurship—and not just because the external need for talent in these spheres is urgent. "Wherever there is success, there is failure," Drucker wrote. "And then it is vitally important for the individual, and equally for the individual's family, to have an area in which he or she can contribute, make a difference and *be somebody*."

Not everyone will find such purpose. People who manage the second half of their lives may always be a minority. The majority may retire on the job and count the years until their actual retirement, Drucker said. "But it is this minority, the men and women who see a long working-life expectancy as an opportunity both for themselves and for society, who will become leaders and models."

Sally Bingham

*Homemaker
to Episcopal Priest*

think the seeds of what I do today were sown out of my strong sense of protecting what I really love, which is the beauty and awe of nature.

I grew up in the country, and I learned about the web of life by watching the birds eat the worms, watching eggs hatch, and animals being born. As a young child, I came to understand that we are part of this web. Everything we do to our natural resources affects us. If we put engine oil in the creek behind the house, it's going to eventually come back and poison us, because it will get into a stream. And then the fish are going to be poisoned, and then we're going to eat the fish. And then, wham, it comes right back.

I've always had a sense of not only the divine in nature, but the interdependence of everything. If one piece is unhealthy, then everything is affected. So when I saw nature being destroyed, and I saw scientific evidence that humans were doing it, there was the call.

I serve as the executive director of The Regeneration Project in San Francisco and I preach at Grace Cathedral [San Francisco's Episcopal cathedral]. The mission of The Regeneration Project is to deepen the connection between ecology and faith. That translates into helping people in the pews, of whatever religion, understand that if you are a faithful religious person who goes to a house of worship on a regular basis and you consider yourself religious, you then have a responsibility to protect what God loves. God loves the Creation, therefore religious people should probably be leading the environmental movement.

We're leading a campaign called "Interfaith Power and Light," which is a religious response to global warming. We ask that our congregations cut their CO_2 emissions. I want people to understand that human behavior is causing global warming. The big cars that we drive, the lights that are on when nobody is in the room, and the computer monitors that are running when nobody is using the computer. There is also a social justice issue. Where are the power plants? They're always in poor neighborhoods. Where are the highest rates of lung disease, cancer, and respiratory problems? In the poor neighborhoods. It's an issue for the faith community. We are called to serve one another, serve the poor, and, by doing that, we serve God.

I've always been a devout Episcopalian, and as I got more and more interested in the fact that we were destroying ourselves, I started asking clergy why the religious community was silent on something that was so important. How can you profess a love for God and pray for a reverence for the earth, then drive away in your Hummer? There was a disconnect between how people were thinking and praying . . . and their behavior.

The clergy that I talked to [in the late 1980s] told me, "Churches are concerned with souls. The environmental community can take care of the trees and the air and the water. Our job is to look after people's souls." And I would say, "Well, if we're not going to look after the trees and the air and the water, we're not going to have any souls to look after." But I didn't get very far. The environment was seen as a department of its own.

Along the way one of these clergy suggested that I go to seminary to understand more about the disconnect I perceived between Christianity and our responsibility for Creation. That appealed to me. I started filling out forms. One of the first questions right up front is, "Where did you go to college?" I hadn't gone to college. I had been raising a family. I got married right out of high school, and I had three children. At that point in time, I had one six-year-old. I had a husband who provided well enough for us that I didn't have to have a paying job. I had an equally important job being with my children. I did a lot of volunteering. But I had not gone to college, and you can't go to seminary unless you've been to college.

So I went to college. I entered the University of San Francisco (USF) in 1985, when one child was a freshman at Berkeley and my youngest was starting elementary school. Off I went as a freshman at age forty-five. I absolutely loved it and graduated in four years. I took a class in religion every semester because USF is a Jesuit school with wonderful teachers and wonderful religious education. I majored in psychology with a minor in religion.

After graduation, I took a year off and then went back and said, "I'm ready to go to seminary now." And they said, "Why seminary?"

The reason was the same as earlier: I wanted to know why the religious community wasn't involved in ecological issues, because everything I had studied and everything I understood told me that we should be leading this movement. It just didn't make sense to me that we weren't. Religion led the civil rights movement, the abolition of slavery, the opening of educational opportunities for women and children.

I went to seminary at the Church Divinity School of the Pacific. In seminary, I met a guy who was very interested in religion and the environment. We started The Regeneration Project together, but we couldn't get any money because we didn't have a focus. We were giving classes, going to Episcopal churches and showing people things they could do. But that wasn't enough. I let The Regeneration Project just sit. I had to graduate from seminary, and then I had to figure out what I was going to do with the rest of my life.

Eventually, we decided to focus on the most important issue concerning ecology that we could find, and that issue was global warming. Coincidentally, California and Massachusetts were deregulating the electrical industry at that time. We thought, let's use this as an opportunity to educate people about where their electricity comes from. And that's what we did. That's when Episcopal Power and Light had its birth. We got Episcopal congregations to buy clean electricity. Then we starting getting calls from people saying, "Can we do this, too? We're Presbyterians. Can we do this, too? We're working for COJO (Coalition for Environment and Jewish Life). Maybe we ought to work together."

We became an interfaith group, which opened a lot of doors and gave us a much bigger audience. We could also show measurable differences. We now ask every congregation to cut energy use, and we ask how each is serving as an example to their parishioners. They tell us, for example, that they put in forty compact fluorescent light bulbs, that they got a new energy efficient refrigerator for their parish hall. They put in sensor lights in the bathrooms so the lights would go out when they weren't in use; they put caulking on the windows so that the air-conditioning wasn't wasted. Then we use a Web site that's been set up for us by the Environmental Protection Agency. We put those numbers in there and calculate just how much CO_2 emission has been prevented from going into the atmosphere. In California, with 130 congregations participating in the program, it is 19,000 tons of CO_2 emissions! Now multiply that by all the other congregations, and you see just what a difference we can make.

I've had challenges in my life, sorting out what's right for me. Marriage was difficult. I've had to face the fact that it's probably not something I'm good at. After I completed my three years of seminary in 1997, after ten years in the process, I got breast cancer. So that was about five or six months of setback. You go through chemotherapy and radiation and you're pretty sick and you can't do much of anything. It's kind of like when you walk through the valley of the shadow of death. But I recovered. And I am completely and 100 percent well.

I didn't have any risk factors for breast cancer—I breast-fed my children. I had them when I was young. I don't smoke. I don't drink a lot. I'm athletic. I eat well. It's not prevalent in my family. It fed my interest in the environment and human health. All this is building a ministry for me. It's all motivating what I now do.

I think you have to keep your heart open to change. You have to be willing to say yes. And I say that out of my own experience—I probably wouldn't have chosen this life, nor would I have planned it out for myself. But as doors opened, and I was willing to walk through them, I've gone on this amazing adventure. At any point, I could have said, "I don't want to do that. It's scary." But I was willing to walk through those doors. (Some of them I had to pound on to get them open!) I think if you have faith, it gives you courage to try things that you're not absolutely sure you're going to be able to accomplish.

CHAPTER SIX

The Encore Society

The U.S. Air Force gave Sandra Sessoms-Penny the chance to escape the life of a migrant farmworker through service to her country. Her encore career as a teacher and school administrator has enabled her to continue to climb, and to continue to serve.

"My mother instilled in me, 'You gotta have a better life.' And, God knows, I wanted a better life than what I saw," says Sessoms-Penny, who as a child helped her parents pick fruit in the citrus groves of South Florida. Without an education, she figured, the only options were working in the fields or cleaning houses. Sessoms-Penny couldn't afford college on her own.

She enlisted during the Vietnam War, as an eighteen-year-old right out of high school and rose from airman first class to senior master sergeant. It took her more than a decade to get her college diploma from a service member's university at Langley Air Force Base, but not nearly that long to follow up with a master's degree in human resources.

She had planned to go to law school when she left the military, but two tries at the law school aptitude exam convinced her otherwise. Teaching was her second choice. As a mom, she had spent a lot of time with kids and thought she had a knack. And she liked the idea that she could give something back, "something that was relevant to them."

Service members are well accustomed to the notion of encore careers, with military careers starting early and typically lasting only twenty to thirty years. That has made the military a model for other industries with ever-shorter career arcs. One of the most innovative career-transition initiatives is the Troops to Teachers program, which since 1993 has helped approximately 9,500 military veterans become public school teachers and administrators. The program reimburses career officers and enlisted personnel up to $5,000 for the cost of the classes and tests they need to get their teaching certificates. A three-year bonus of up to $10,000 provides an incentive for Troops teachers to work in high-need schools and stick with it.

Troops to Teachers is itself the product of an encore career. When J. H. "Jack" Hexter, a history professor, was forced to retire from Yale at age sixty-five, he transferred to Washington University in St. Louis, where he taught for another fifteen years. There, he recognized an opportunity in the retirement of thousands of soldiers in their forties and early fifties that accompanied the downsizing of the military at the end of the Cold War. With a little incentive, Hexter thought, service members might help fill the chronic need for public school teachers. Hexter worked for six years to gain support for his idea, finally convincing Senator John Danforth to secure federal funding for the program in the 1993 defense spending bill—a year before Hexter died.

Sessoms-Penny was among the program's earliest recruits, and Troops to Teachers paid for a second master's degree in education. She was quickly hired as a middle-school teacher. "Having my education paid for and then finding a job teaching right away and being able to stay in that job and just grow in that position, I figure it's divine intervention," she says. She now serves as assistant principal of a 500-student rural school, Windsor High School in Isle of Wight County, Virginia.

In her fifties, Sessoms-Penny isn't yet halfway through what she expects to be a twenty-four-year career in education, two years longer than her military career. At Windsor, her experience helps encourage students to expand their horizons, and her military experience helps her get things done.

"The military teaches discipline, teamwork, planning, organizing, getting things done in a timely manner, keeping the objectives in mind," she says. "Military folks, we're used to being a part of something and making something go. We say, 'This has got to be done, there's no way around it, what are your ideas?' Then we get everybody's ideas heading in the same direction."

She is now paying her own way through a Ph.D. program at George Washington University. Her dissertation on Troops to Teachers' role in filling teacher shortages found that age and experience helped prepare veterans, not only for the classroom but for a chronically underappreciated profession.

"In the military, too, you know, you are standing in defense of folks who don't know you and don't respect you or what you're doing," she states. "And it's the same thing in the school system. Not everybody supports what you do or how you do it, but you know that it must be done."

Virtues and Necessities Redux

Think back fifty years, before Sun City, Leisure World, and the Golden Years, when retirees were consigned to a roleless role, shoved to the sidelines of society.

Then, seemingly overnight, a new norm emerged. Social Security, corporate pensions, and Medicare all played an important role in establishing the financial underpinnings for the retired, while employers and policymakers worked overtime to usher older workers out of the labor force. But it took more than government policies or economic incentives to reshape life plans. It took a shift in thinking that equated retirement with leisure, and it took brilliant social invention.

Together they turned the most rejected stage of life into one so coveted that millions scrimped and saved during their working years to underwrite this cherished future promise. Del Webb sold the dream, along with some real estate. Financial services and insurance companies sold the dream, along with the pensions and annuities to finance it. And before too long, people bought the dream. Rather than dreading retirement, they rushed toward it, as early as possible. The push became a pull.

The change was so complete that things seemed to have always been that way, and it remained thus for half a century.

Now a new combination of forces is impelling change. The necessity today is to encourage people to continue to work in ways that truly use their talents to support the economy as well as themselves. It is essential that those who have a strong need and desire to work in this new way have every chance to realize that objective and every opportunity to use their accumulated human and social capital in areas where it matters most.

In this context, a nascent but growing collection of innovative organizations, individual entrepreneurs, and other leading-edge groups is stepping forward to change the landscape, demonstrating the potential of the encore career.

Troops to Teachers is among the most innovative of these new inventions—combining policy innovation and common-sense logic with compelling results. And there are others.

In New York City, a fledgling organization called ReServe connects experienced and educated individuals who have finished their midlife careers to meaningful work opportunities in the public and nonprofit sectors. ReServe helps place employees in areas of grinding human resource need: in community justice initiatives that help those navigating the criminal justice system, in understaffed school libraries and after-school programs, and in the executive offices of public and nonprofit institutions.

Nationally, more than 2,000 members of Experience Corps work with 20,000 children in more than twenty cities to help them succeed in school. Those Experience Corps members who commit to working fifteen hours a week receive a small monthly stipend to cover their expenses. The individuals typically stay for years in Experience Corps, turning what started out as a short Peace Corps–like engagement into an extended encore career focused on public education. The majority of Experience Corps members are African American women and men, many of whom do not have a college degree. And Experience Corps members not only work part-time but get summers off, showing that encore careers can be just as flexible as retail bridge jobs, and even more rewarding.

Faith-based organizations and corporations alike are getting in on the action. Texas businessman Bob Buford realized that for many Christians, midlife—or "halftime" as he calls it—is a natural point for introspection and life change. It's a time to take stock and consider a career change to do work that improves the world and provides personal fulfillment as well as spiritual growth and "Kingdom-building," in Buford's view. In addition to the Leadership Network, which fosters innovation and spreads new ideas to Christian churches, Buford created Halftime to "mobilize and equip high-capacity business/professional leaders to convert their faith into action and effective results," in the form of changed lives and healthier communities.

Corporations are beginning to see opportunities for themselves and their communities. IBM Corp. has launched Transition to Teaching, a program that helps senior IBM scientists and engineers get their teaching certificates and find student-teaching opportunities and ultimately jobs. In addition to grants of up to $15,000 per employee to defray the costs of schooling, IBM provides employees with up to four months of paid time off to fulfill their student-teaching requirements.

"People aren't ready for retirement at fifty-two or fifty-three years old," IBM's average retirement age, says Stan Litow, president of the IBM International Foundation and a former deputy superintendent of New York City schools. "People want to use the opportunity of a second career to do something that is meaningful."

The IBM program is one of several demonstrating the value of tapping second-act boomers in transforming education. The Broad Academy for superintendents, funded by Los Angeles billionaire Eli Broad, targets CEOs and senior executives from business, military, government, and education backgrounds to lead urban public school systems. The idea is to deepen and widen the pool of those who want to go into superintendent and other school leadership positions.

Participants go through a rigorous ten-month executive

management program covering necessary skills in finance, management, operations, organizational systems, and education—all while keeping their current jobs. Tuition costs are covered by the Academy. Graduates benefit from an extensive support network and can expect to be placed in superintendent positions or senior cabinet level positions within eighteen months.

At the local level, Next Chapter projects, assisted by Civic Ventures, have been established in dozens of communities nationwide. Led by community-based organizations like libraries and community colleges, the projects help adults moving beyond their midlife careers make the transition to their encore phase. Animated by the twin themes of *connection* and *direction,* Next Chapter helps people in the second half of life explore their options, set a course, and hook up with service opportunities, including encore careers. If retooled skills or new credentials are called for, people are pointed to a variety of learning options.

In Tempe, Arizona, for example, the project is housed in a new café on the first floor of the Tempe public library, which serves as a one-stop resource for people of all ages planning their "next chapters." At The Connections Café, visitors can get an infusion of caffeine while searching for a paid job at a local nonprofit, attend life-planning workshops, stop in at the Experience Corps office to learn about tutoring at the local elementary school, or compare notes with others in the midst of their own transitions to a new phase of life.

All over the country there are encouraging and increasing

signs of the encore career ferment. The YMCA of Greater Rochester, New York, is emerging as a model nonprofit recruiter of individuals over fifty, who now comprise 20 percent of the Y's workforce. The Y offers a set of creative options, including flex time, compressed work schedules, job sharing, and telecommuting. The Partnership for Public Service in 2007 launched the FedExperience project in recognition that close to half the federal workers will be eligible for retirement over the next five years, including nearly three-fourths of senior managers. The Partnership hopes to help the public sector do a much better job of recruiting leading-edge boomers from other sectors to second careers in an array of critical government positions. New Directions, a for-profit outplacement firm for senior executives and professionals in Boston, has developed a specialty in helping its clients find encore opportunities in the social sector as part of developing a "portfolio life." The nonprofit human resource group BridgeStar is targeting boomers (along with several other promising groups) in its efforts to stem the leadership deficit in the nonprofit sector.

To be sure, there are still not enough encore career opportunities for all the people who will want them. But thousands of aging boomers are not waiting for a job posting to tackle tough social challenges. By identifying and implementing an innovative solution to a problem, they are also creating their own career opportunities. Social entrepreneurship, once thought to be mainly the province of the young, turns out to be a path to vibrant encore careers for many people.

One indicator of the growth in this arena is The Purpose Prize, another initiative of Civic Ventures, which identifies, highlights, and invests in social innovators who have started their new projects after age fifty. The prospect of five $100,000 prizes, along with a range of smaller awards, attracted 1,500 nominees in the first year.

W. Wilson Goode Sr., who returned to divinity school after serving as the mayor of Philadelphia, was one of the first Purpose Prize winners. In 2000, at age sixty-one, Goode agreed to lead Amachi, a national organization that links mentors with children whose parents are in prison. Experts estimate that without intervention, 70 percent of these children would also end up in jail. Goode rallied pastors in predominantly African American communities to encourage their congregants to be mentors, and he went into prisons to rally incarcerated parents to stand up for their children's future. Today, 240 Amachi-style programs in forty-eight states have helped 30,000 children. Last year, the *Philadelphia Inquirer* named Goode its Citizen of the Year.

Other winners include: Barney Flynn, a farmer-turned-environmentalist who has helped restore thousands of acres of riverfront wildlife habitat; Martha Rollins, an antique dealer who is providing job opportunities for ex-offenders; and Herb Sturz, the co-founder of ReServe. Many of these entrepreneurs, such as Sturz and ReServe's co-founder, former *New York Times Magazine* editor and Pulitzer Prize–winner Jack Rosenthal, are using their talents to create pathways for their peers.

Such examples are spurring other funders to invest in second-half social innovators as well. Ashoka, an international fellowship program that established social entrepreneurship as a career path primarily for young people, last year named Charlotte Frank, in her sixties, as a fellow, as well as a number of other fellows in the second half of life. After a high-profile career in government, Frank founded the Transition Network, a resource for women over fifty planning the next phase of their lives. And Ashoka's founder, Bill Drayton, continues to add to his own remarkable string of social innovations as he moves into his sixties.

Enabling the Encore Society

As encouraging as these signs may be, they only go part of the way toward addressing the scale of the transformation required to turn the aging of the boomers from a crisis into an opportunity for personal and social renewal. And for all of Peter Drucker's good counsel about managing oneself, self-management alone is necessary but not sufficient. How can we go beyond individuals one at a time trying to navigate the new terrain? How can we go beyond the current patchwork of opportunities? How can we meet this new generation of individuals halfway, and in time for the population explosion in front of us? Answering these and other key questions requires first putting the current situation into a larger context.

For more than fifty years, we have treated older adults much the way we have treated farmers: Just as we pay farmers not to grow crops, we've made it worthwhile for people to stop working. We have said: If you agree to leave your job at sixty-five, and earlier if at all possible, we'll provide financial incentives and security, we'll provide pathways and support to leave, and we'll dress it all in a definition of success that centers on leisure and recreation, in the dream of the Golden Years.

That implicit contract, which stretches back to the Depression, was animated by a belief that individuals sought freedom from work, and that we were all better off if they left the productive sphere.

Now the opposite is true. Study after study shows that individuals want to, hope to, and need to continue working at the age when previous generations retired. And we need them to as well, as labor and talent shortages crimp key sectors such as education, health care, nonprofits, public employment, and even the clergy, all of which could reap an experience dividend from the enormous human-capital investments that were made in the boomer generation. Our fiscal health requires longer working lives, and our physical and mental health may benefit as well.

A new deal is needed. The great challenge for the American economy and for American society over the next half century, for individual happiness and generational solidarity, for labor market efficiency and fiscal solvency, will be to develop a new social compact that inverts the old arrangement that pushed and pulled people out of the labor market.

Imagine this new compact: If you sign up for a significant new stage of work, and if you invest in and prepare for this phase, society will meet you halfway. We'll help clear away the barriers and obstacles that make continued work difficult and complicated. We'll develop better pathways to a significant second career. We'll help you find engagement that truly uses your skills, experience, and know-how, and we'll focus on opportunities where your assets are genuinely needed. We'll even build in a break to help you catch your breath and retool for what's next, and we'll make work flexible enough to adapt to life's realities.

This new compact offers the opportunity to get work right, in a way most people don't have a chance to in midlife. In short, people will have a chance at an encore career, a body of work that offers continued income, identity, social connection, and the promise of purpose and significance in the second half of life. For some, this will mean working in the social sector, in such areas as education, health care, and the environment, or it might mean creating or joining a socially responsible business. For others, it will mean work that balances personal fulfillment with social impact more broadly.

Realizing this vision will take more than promising pilot programs and fiddling around the edges of policy change. The magnitude of what is occurring is so great, the consequences so vast, and the obstacles sufficiently significant that only big thinking and bold action will do the trick. It will further require acting quickly. Although the new norm for the period opening up between midlife and retirement is currently up for grabs, it won't remain that way for long, as myriad interests rush in with their own designs on the boomer population.

Such a new social compact will require a comprehensive set of changes, in attitudes as much as in policies, in imagination as much as in investments.

THINK ENCORE. The new stage of life is something uniquely new, not a rerun. Sixty isn't the new forty, or the new thirty. It's the new sixty. The key question for individuals entering this stage is: What do you want to do now that you've grown up?

The persistence of a "retirement" mindset even among those who claim to be reinventing it has hampered the development of new approaches and opportunities. In social science terms, it's a classic example of a "structural lag" that keeps cultural conceptions and social institutions stuck in an earlier era even as realities change dramatically. We need to be liberated from artificial notions such as "retirement age" and the oxymoronic concept "working in retirement." We need to be liberated, too, from such dreary and bloodless phrases as "older workers" and "mature workers." This is not a call for euphemisms, but rather for precision and accuracy. The truth is that the vast majority of individuals in this stage of life are neither retired nor anything approximating old— and these trends will only accelerate in the coming years.

It's time to create a new category of thinking and a new language: the encore stage and the encore career. The sooner we recognize that we are entering fresh territory, shaping a new stage of life and work between the middle years and true retirement and old age, the more quickly progress will come in grasping the possibilities of this new period.

The expanded time horizon of the encore career changes everything. Planning for a ten-, twenty-, or thirty-year stage of life is different, qualitatively as well as quantitatively, from planning for a five-year retirement. As that notion takes hold broadly, all sorts of customs and institutions will undergo similar qualitative change.

We need to market the possibilities of "the second half of work." Individuals approaching this phase face an identity crisis as they struggle for a vision and the words to describe their current situation. Just as important, potential employers need to understand the encore career, to realize that these individuals are neither passing through nor phasing out but rather embarking on a new body of work for a time span long enough to make investing in them worth the effort.

CLEAR THE DEBRIS. Many of the policies developed in earlier decades to usher workers out of the workforce remain on the books, providing perverse disincentives that contradict the new social goal of encouraging people to keep working in ways that use their experience and are personally fulfilling. We need to get rid of them, along with outmoded conceptions that devalue talent and experience.

For many people in their mid-sixties, not working pays

almost as much as working, the result of a set of "taxes" on work in this stage that are levied on top of traditional income and other taxes. Taking all factors into consideration, one study found the implicit tax on a typical worker rises from 14 percent at age fifty-five to 50 percent at age seventy. Removing disincentives for working, such as reduced Social Security and other retirement benefits, would encourage individuals at this stage to improve their own financial security as well as the nation's economic health.

Another sensible reform would be to permit workers over sixty-five to opt out of additional payroll deductions for Social Security. Why pay, when you could be getting paid instead? Elimination of the payroll tax would be an effective wage increase, an additional incentive for continued work. And eliminating the employer's portion would lower the cost of employing these workers, making them more attractive to hire and retain.

The list goes on. For example, provisions of pension law now make it complicated for workers over fifty to dip into their employee benefits before they completely leave the workforce, limiting the possibilities for new kinds of flexible work arrangements. Other provisions require employers to pay equal benefits to all workers who log more than 1,000 hours a year, giving employers a reason to hold part-timers under that level. Letting employers offer pro-rated levels of benefits would increase their ability to introduce flexible work arrangements.

Some of the debris is pure prejudice. *Ageism in America*, a major study by the International Longevity Center, documented the persistence of age discrimination in health care, nursing homes, emergency services, and the media, as well as in the workplace. "Retirement rates are higher than they might otherwise be; older unemployed people have greater difficulty finding work; the skills of older workers are underutilized; older workers are passed over for promotion or omitted from training programs—all, in great part, because of the existence of ageism among employers," the study concluded.

SWEETEN THE POT. Carrots tend to be more appealing than sticks, for people as well as horses. We should give workers earlier, not later, access to tax-advantaged savings, corporate pensions, and benefits such as health care. Additional financial flexibility to launch an encore career or renegotiate a current one would make working longer about choice, not punishment.

To date, most of the changes in the equation around longer working lives have taken the form of sticks rather than carrots. Cutbacks in retiree pension and health benefits raise the "cost" of retirement and serve to keep people working longer.

But incentives may work even better than disincentives. For example, under current law, individuals can increase their monthly income for life simply by postponing the date at which they claim Social Security payments for three years after their "normal" retirement age. Future payments increase by 8 percent a year for up to three years, producing a lifetime monthly bonus of up to 24 percent. A study by the Federal Reserve found that the bonus has been effective in spurring people to work longer. Extending it beyond three years could make it even more effective.

Still, it is essential to underscore that we need more than discrete incentives. We need a powerful package that backs up a new vision for work—for employers, employees, and society more broadly.

EXPAND HEALTH COVERAGE. Proposals for universal health insurance coverage were once greeted with snorts of derision as utopian or socialist pipe dreams. But such plans have now risen to the top of many states' political agenda.

Coverage for children has been the most common beachhead for advocates seeking to incrementally shrink the ranks of the uninsured. But aging boomers can tag along on the movement. Fear of losing coverage keeps many workers tethered to jobs they are otherwise ready to leave, inhibiting their ability to launch encore careers. According to the Kaiser Family Foundation, those over fifty but not yet eligible for Medicare at sixty-five face the hardest time getting affordable individual health insurance because of age-related premiums and restrictions on preexisting conditions.

At the same time, higher health care costs for older workers represent a direct disincentive for hiring. The costs of providing health coverage for workers over fifty-five can be as much as twice the cost for workers younger than forty-four. The consulting firm Towers Perrin found that employees between fifty and sixty-five use from 1.4 to 2.2 times as much health care as workers in their thirties and forties.

The point is not lost on employers. A survey by Boston College's Center for Retirement Research found that more than 40 percent of employers say older workers are more expensive than younger ones (although they also see them as equally or more productive, partially offsetting the increased costs). Another study found that firms that offer health insurance are less likely to hire older workers than firms that do not.

Short of a true universal plan, there are various ways to increase health insurance coverage for workers in their fifties and sixties. One proposal is to allow individuals to buy into Medicare early, at a rate similar to group insurance policies that provide similar benefits and without regard to preexisting conditions. Another option is to extend the time period for so-called COBRA coverage, which allows former employees to pay their own premiums for group coverage under an employer's plan, until individuals are eligible for Medicare.

There is one simple fix: Change federal rules that require employers to provide workers' coverage under their employer group plans. Allowing workers over sixty-five to get their coverage through Medicare would reduce employers' costs, creating an incentive to hire these workers.

MORE THAN A BREAK. It's time for a national sabbatical for individuals completing the first half of midlife work and beginning to contemplate their encore phase.

To start, many Americans entering the second half of life are exhausted. Even if they aren't working in "extreme jobs" requiring seventy or eighty hours a week, the combined weight of already long hours on the job and the duties of parenting leave women, and quite a few men, panting by the time they hit their early to mid-fifties. This is not the best state from which to launch an encore career—and beyond the exhaustion, there is the simple fact that few have had much time to think about what to do next, much less try on different roles. Yet that question looms large as the middle years far outlast the length of most first careers.

Mary Catherine Bateson, recognizing this problem, suggests something akin to the "gap year"—the European institution whereby many young people take a break between high school and college, or between college and their first job—for individuals in their fifties and sixties. In Bateson's view, this time might be used to go back to school or to spend a year or two in service to the nation. Just as adding an atrium to a house radiates light to the rest of the rooms, a midlife atrium that raises the ceiling on possibilities will radiate opportunities for all stages of life, she writes.

Individuals need the chance both to think about "what's next" and to try on various possibilities, ideally through internship-like experience akin to the way medical students rotate through various specialties. Equally important, there's the need to catch up developmentally. We all know, for example, that young people head off to college every bit as much to figure out *who* they are going to be next as to prepare for *what* they are going to do next. A parallel transition is needed between the end of midlife and the onset of the encore stage.

INTRODUCING THE ENCORE FELLOWS. National service programs have traditionally been focused on young people. It's time to stop overlooking the biggest source of people ready to ask what they can do for their country.

In a Ford Foundation study nearly two decades ago, former U.S. Navy secretary Richard Danzig and Harvard policy expert Peter Szanton contended that those over fifty have more to give and more to gain from national service than any other group. The Progressive Policy Institute has proposed creation of a national Boomer Corps, which would provide tuition vouchers and other incentives for those who provide several years of national service.

Let's support a broad cross-section of talented individuals in their desire to serve their communities and the nation by creating flexible, practical Encore Fellowships. Those selected as Encore Fellows would be given vouchers to enable them to approach nonprofit groups or public agencies for an internship. The vouchers would underwrite a stipend for the Encore Fellow while also providing funds to the organization for training. The program would be patterned on the best features of the White House Fellows Program and the Coro Fellows. Organizations would compete to get smart, talented, Encore Fellows.

John Gomperts, president of Civic Ventures (and formerly chief of staff of the Corporation for National Service, the parent of the AmeriCorps program), argues that this model would overcome twin obstacles to the encore career. "Individuals seeking to make a major commitment to service and good work often suffer from a lack of access to and knowledge of appropriate career opportunities," he observes. "And just as people are not certain what they want, organizations are not certain that they can make the required hiring commitment."

Young people have had internships, fellowships, and other support systems that provide opportunities for career exploration and give organizations an inexpensive labor pool and a concrete way to engage young people. The Encore Fellows program, Gomperts contends, would create a similar pathway and infrastructure for people who have completed their midlife careers and want to enter into a new period of work for the greater good.

The program could start as a federal pilot program for as few as 1,000 Encore Fellows in early years, but the real goal should be 100,000 or more. We would expect the Encore Fellows model to be copied and extended by state and local governments, community and national foundations, and critically, private-sector employers who see a sound business case for helping employees nearing the culmination of one career make the transition to nonprofit or public-sector jobs.

HIGHEST EDUCATION. We are poised for an encore revolution in higher education. Thirty years ago, institutions such as Elderhostel in America and the University of the Third Age in the United Kingdom broke down the notion that higher education was just for the young. However, these efforts focused mostly on self-development and learning for its own sake, in many ways pursuing a higher form of the leisure ethic assumed to accompany retirement.

But what about adapting higher education for those who need retooling to launch the next phase of their working lives? Most individuals are forced to jump through the same hoops as an eighteen-year-old or a twenty-two-year-old. But devoting four years to school at age fifty-eight is a much bigger commitment than it was forty years earlier—and often an unnecessary one. As a result, Rosabeth Kanter, a noted Harvard Business School professor and social scientist, proposes an entirely new form of higher education for aging boomers.

Her proposal, for SAIL (School for Advanced Institutional Leadership), won Kanter and her colleagues, Rakesh Khurana and Nitin Nohria, *Fast Company*'s 2006 Fast 50 award for a "blue-hair university." This characterization aside, Kanter's proposal is anything but musty. She suggests a leadership initiative for the most motivated and accomplished individuals who combine an interdisciplinary academic course with a thesis focused on how they plan to change the world. They would earn an advanced leadership degree for their efforts.

Proposals for revamping higher education are appearing

in many different forms. For example, Washington University professor Nancy Morrow Howell suggests an "executive MSW" (Master of Social Work) program for second-career individuals with considerable life experience and the desire to enter the human services sector. A recent fortieth reunion gathering of Wharton School graduates from the University of Pennsylvania generated a similar notion—a summer intensive institute helping business and law school graduates make the transition to the nonprofit sector.

Community colleges have a big role to play. Gateway Community College in Phoenix is proposing a new Boomer Transition Center focused on helping fifty- and sixty-something individuals make a career transition into education, health care, or social work roles.

How could we enable all of these educational opportunities to happen on a grand scale, and with a focus on helping individuals prepare for jobs where they are most needed? One possibility is a reverse GI Bill. The GI Bill was built on the concept of rewarding service with educational opportunity. It was one of the great policy achievements of the twentieth century. For people who have completed their midlife careers and now want to move into work or service in the nonprofit sector, education, health care, or other important fields facing labor shortages, a reverse GI Bill could provide similar benefits.

Many people who want to move into these high-need professions will require a period of training or education. Some might need to obtain a credential or degree. The student-loan approach may not be practical for people in their middle years. A reverse GI Bill, patterned after ROTC and Public Health Service Corps approaches, would help midlife individuals pay for education and training; the beneficiaries would then repay the educational support through a period of service in a needed profession. One year of education or training could be repaid through one or two years of service or work.

Government funding could be greatly enhanced through investments by individuals themselves in their encore careers. These investments could be promoted through simple reforms, for example, by expanding the approved uses of tax-advantaged individual retirement accounts and 401Ks to include such necessary transition costs as education, training, or health coverage.

Some individuals approaching this juncture are not waiting for legislative action and are financing their return to school with tax-advantaged college savings accounts that were intended for younger students. Such 529 accounts (they're named for the section of the IRS code that created them) allow investments to be withdrawn tax-free as long as the proceeds are spent on higher education. The funds can be used for business and computer classes, as well as for nursing or teaching programs, as long as the course is accredited at a college or vocational school eligible for federal student-aid programs, which includes virtually all postsecondary schools. They are likely to catch on quickly if financial service firms turn their marketing toward "Encore 529s."

REVAMP THE WORKPLACE. A few simple innovations will go a long way toward meeting the needs of individuals who want to have the greatest impact but are unwilling to continue to turn their lives completely over to work.

Job sharing, telecommuting, extended vacation time, and a raft of other nifty ideas can be as adeptly applied to encore careers as to retail "bridge jobs." As already stated, Experience Corps is one such example—providing full-time, half-time, and part-time opportunities, while also enabling most members to take the summers off. A very different example is Fritz Schwarz's role of senior counsel at the Brennan Center for Justice at NYU. Outside the traditional hierarchy, alongside leading high-impact litigation efforts, a major part of his role involves mentoring and guiding young public-interest lawyers, not only exposing them to advanced legal skills but helping them to gain a deeper sense of what it means to be a crusading lawyer.

There are immense opportunities for such new and flexible roles in the nonprofit world. Although most nonprofits have a CEO and a CFO, they are often particularly thin in skilled positions in marketing, human resources, legal counseling, and communications. At the same time, an unprecedented number of women and men, including an extraordinary number of MBAs with precisely these skills, are approaching the end of their midlife careers in the corporate sector. Many are seeking new purpose and greater flexibility in the next phase of their working lives, while desiring to use the skills they have acquired over many decades. Why not consider helping them transition into the nonprofit sector, through inventing not only new pathways but new flexible management roles? The result might be not only more fulfilled workers but a social sector that is far more effective.

Another needed change transcends sectors. As Peter Capelli, a professor of management at the University of Pennsylvania's Wharton School and director of its Center on Human Resources, argues: "Many employers are stuck on an old principle of human resources, that to be fair means treating everyone in the organization the same." This principle means that no group gets special or differential treatment, and it grows out of legal as well as ethical concerns. But it can present significant barriers to engaging the talents of those in the second half of work.

Capelli sees these barriers as surmountable, but he suggests an immediate fix: "New institutions in the labor market provide a more immediate solution," he writes. "Temporary help agencies and staffing firms have begun to develop specialties in supplying older workers. An organization that is interested in engaging older workers but worries about conflicts and problems with their own employment practices can hire older workers as temps or contractors. The workers remain employees of the temp and staffing agencies, which handle all the potentially messy legal issues. The result is one of the rare 'win-win' situations for the modern workforce."

INVEST IN INNOVATION. Twenty years ago under the first Bush administration, a quasi-public commission pumped over $50 million a year into efforts such as City Year and Teach for America, turning small pilot programs into national institutions, which in turn have helped change the definition of success for young people coming out of college. The same effort could be made today with innovative pilot programs aimed at changing the definition of success for people coming out of midlife careers.

What if nonprofits like Teach for America, which already has an infrastructure for introducing young people to public education, adapted to this new audience with the support of such an encore investment fund? There is evidence that new investment might lure many of the most creative social-sector organizations into this arena.

Much value would also come from expanding and adapting groundbreaking vehicles already in existence, beginning with the remarkable Troops to Teachers program. Federal employees, for example, receive an excellent package after thirty years of federal service, allowing many to retire from the federal government in their mid-fifties with decades of potential productive public service left. The Troops to Teachers model should be adapted for other federal agencies and should be extended to other high-need areas.

It's even worth considering ways to encourage individuals to invest in the encore careers of their peers. Consider this possibility: Affluent individuals able to forgo Social Security checks for a year or more could choose to redirect all or part of their benefits to a social investment fund that could be, for example, dedicated to deploying the time and talents of aging boomers on challenges facing youth. Such a "Generational Challenge" fund could be administered by community foundations and used to attract hundreds of thousands of experienced adults into schools, after-school activities, mentorship programs, and other youth-development initiatives, fulfilling Social Security's original goal of broad social progress by reconnecting the generations in shared purpose.

Such an initiative already exists, albeit locally and on a small scale, in the form of Hope for Generations in Denver, Colorado. Jerry Conover, a successful trial lawyer, decided the Social Security checks he began receiving at sixty-five were nice but not necessary. He had a part-time mediation practice, and his real estate investments allowed him to live comfortably without a monthly $1,500 Social Security check. In 2002, at age sixty-eight, Conover and a few friends started redirecting their Social Security payments into a fund to address the education and health needs of children.

Now, the fund includes former Democratic governor Dick Lamm and a Coors family heir, as well as retired schoolteachers and social workers who contribute more modest amounts. In its first three years, Hope for Generations, administered by the Denver Foundation, invested $250,000 in eleven organizations serving the needs of young children in Colorado. Conover hopes to take Hope for Generations nationwide, to "create a new 'social contract' between generations."

THE ENCORE BILL. A coherent and ambitious package of policies to clear the path to new engagement and contribution for America's largest generation could be the nation's first great social achievement of the twenty-first century.

Such a package would likely more than recoup its costs. It would have to be an omnibus bill, including new incentives, the removal of barriers, support for innovation, adaptation of existing institutions, and most fundamentally, a new approach to public policy for this stage of life.

We'll need to think big. In the aftermath of World War II, we faced the prospect of millions of Americans returning from the war, many of them from abroad. The challenge was to reintegrate these individuals into productive new roles. Failure to do so would not only have constituted a betrayal of their service to the country but an extraordinary loss of human talent—and a potential source of great social dislocation. In response, we created the GI Bill, and the result was an economic and social windfall, including greater social mobility.

Today, we face the prospect of tens of millions of boomers moving through their fifties and into their sixties. Some are crossing from military life to civilian roles, much like their predecessors after World War II. For most, it's a divide in the life cycle, a move from well-established terrain to a new phase of life and work that remains poorly defined but will last for decades. If they fail to navigate this transition successfully, if they are left at loose ends, underemployed, lacking purpose, feeling diminished and betrayed, the results could be disastrous for the economy, for society, and for individuals.

Although public policy will not single-handedly shape the outcome of this challenge, it can play an important role. In the absence of a thoughtful policy agenda, many will still find their footing in the new stage. But those who do will likely be the most affluent, educated, and connected, buying their way out of the difficulties. There is already an upsurge in transition services for those willing and able to pay for them, from expensive leadership and transition training programs (Harvard's now defunct Odyssey Program cost $15,000) to individual career or life counseling at $100-plus an hour.

Lost in the free-market version of this future are people like Sandra Sessoms-Penny or the members of Experience Corps. Through public policies like Troops to Teachers and public and private funding of programs like Experience Corps, as well as through government support of community college and state university programs enabling individuals to prepare for encore work, we can democratize the new dream for the second half of life. For many, it can be an opportunity for social mobility, a chance to pursue a profession that was out of reach when they entered the work force.

Creating the Future

This book began with contrasting visions of America in 2030. In one, a self-centered wave of boomers is taking America to the cleaners. Put prematurely out to pasture, underused, and contributing little to the economy or society, they instead are leveraging their political might to get their own—at the expense of younger generations and posterity itself.

In the other, America is realizing an experience dividend, recapturing the staggering investment in human and social capital present in the biggest generation in American history, as tens of millions of boomers use their know-how in ways that are both needed and contribute to a new sense of meaning and purpose. The country is riding a high wave of individual and social renewal.

According to science fiction writer William Gibson, "The future is already here—it's just unevenly distributed." In this case, both futures are already here. One need only pick up the papers to read about the dystopian prospect playing out: Labor shortages opening up in key areas; the fiscal situation worsening; more and more Americans thrust into the second half of life at loose ends, cut out of the productive sphere entirely or shunted into jobs that write off their talent and experience. The result is a growing sense of sourness, lost opportunity, supply missing demand, and vice versa. It's the future that makes no sense.

The previous chapters tell the story of a different prospect, also here and present—a future in which work works, experience counts, and the second half has become the new crown of life. Individuals in this second half are working in ways that produce only wins. From all walks of life, they are earning needed income, paying taxes, using what they know, contributing to the greater good, and living lives that matter.

They stand at the intersection of two of the most important developments of our time: the dramatic lengthening of working lives and the growing realization that we must pull together to make a better world.

To those large impulses they bring large numbers, the scale needed to bring about great transformation.

With so much to gain, it would seem that the predominance of this future, and the society that makes sense for all generations, will be easy and automatic—the inevitable result of inexorable logic. But demography is not destiny, for bad or for good. Realizing the society that makes sense, that not only muddles through but manages to break through to a better way of living and working, will require more than logic. It will take leadership.

As Peter Drucker famously remarked, "The best way to predict the future is to create it." Put another way, à la *Pogo*, we have met the leaders, and they are us. Our personal choices will determine the larger choice we face about the future, whether we ride the great windfall in health and longevity to a better world or let it slip away.

Some well-known figures are already answering this leadership imperative. In 2006, Bill Gates announced at age fifty that he planned to leave his day job at Microsoft Corporation in two years to work full time on global health, education, and other urgent social issues. The intellectual and operational challenges, not to mention the political ones, would be even more daunting than those of selling software and the payoff potentially more important. Gates's move signaled that it was not only acceptable, but expected that a hard-nosed business pragmatist should become a practical idealist, and should do it now.

Whereas Gates had once expected to make such a move at perhaps sixty, his interests and the urgency of the challenges accelerated his timeline. Gates made clear he was launching a new career phase, one that was going to be characterized by social entrepreneurship, a deep engagement distinct from the more distant late-life philanthropy typical of many wealthy individuals in the past, and that the new phase might be as long or longer than the Microsoft years. In announcing this new trajectory, Gates stated simply: "The change we announced today is not a retirement. It's a reordering of my priorities."

As Sherry Lansing, then chairman of Paramount Pictures, neared sixty, she began to plan the next stage of her life. Before she got into movies, Lansing had been a high school teacher in the tough Watts neighborhood of Los Angeles, and she was driven to get back to her roots. "I asked myself, 'What is it that really gives me pleasure?'" Lansing says. "The answer is giving back."

Lansing was a longtime member of the board of Teach for America, the spectacularly successful national service program that attracts bright college graduates into a stint in the classroom. Lansing wrote a piece for the *Huffington Post*, Arianna Huffington's blog, calling for a similar initiative to mobilize aging boomers to serve as teachers in urban schools. She was off and running.

Lansing led the panel of judges that selected the Purpose Prize winners and is working with Beverly Ryder and others on an initiative to put the time and talent of boomers to work for the Los Angeles Unified School District. More broadly, she is launching what she terms the "prime time" movement built around the idea that individuals in the second half of life, dedicated to service, constitute one of America's great hopes for the future.

The importance of this emerging leadership among prominent movers and shakers is essential and heartening. The journeys of Beverly Ryder and Ed Speedling, Jacqueline Khan and Robert Chambers, Sandra Sessoms-Penny and Sally Bingham, and numerous others, show that there are many paths to such leadership. From all walks of life, moving into fields as diverse as nursing and the ministry, some choosing the path of social entrepreneurship, these individuals often feel they are alone, even out of step, making choices that are merely individual in nature.

But choosing the encore path, these innovators are electing to be at the vanguard of something large and significant. They are choosing to lead, to create the future, to answer Drucker's challenge. By breaking through to new roles they are like the women of the last generation who defied convention and opened doors for the many millions coming quickly on their heels.

The stakes are every bit as great today. The opportunity is rising and the time is right. The future is calling.

What are we waiting for?

Your Encore

An Introductory Guide to Finding Your Encore Career

When you're using your business acumen to help people struggling with mental illness, get homeless youth off the street, or work with abused kids . . . you may go home frustrated over work . . . . But you never go home wondering why you went to work in the first place; that's front and center all the time.

Jim McClurg, Social Enterprise Alliance

What will you do for your encore career?

It's tough to change jobs after fifty, let alone careers. Those who have tried have found that reinventing one's worklife calls for an act of imagination, at any age.

And yet there are people out there who are doing it. The trailblazers you've read about in this book—and those you know in your own lives—are finding important, satisfying work, albeit often after bumpy rides. Their efforts are making it a little less bumpy for the rest of us, as they are showcasing a wide variety of paths and techniques for finding encore careers and convincing employers that experienced people dedicated to making the world a better place make excellent employees.

But there aren't enough of these trailblazers. And they have not been able to eradicate age discrimination or create a raft of flexible jobs in the nonprofit and public sectors, nor have they made continuing education and retraining commonplace and affordable or solved the health insurance problem.

At least not yet.

That means you're likely in for a bumpy ride, too. This guide is intended to get you started in your thinking. Warning: It's still early in this movement, and many individuals, organizations, and employers are just waking up to new realities about the life course and the job market. Those in midlife and beyond who are looking for purposeful work will need to be patient. More and better resources and opportunities are surely coming.

One thing about successful encore careerists, though— they don't wait around.

Getting Started

There are a lot of ways to get this process started. You could start by talking to your friends and family—or your financial planner. You could find inspiration in a copy of Rick Warren's *The Purpose-Driven Life* or a well-thumbed copy of Richard Nelson Bolles's *What Color Is Your Parachute?* You could spend time scouring the Web or visiting a life coach for ideas and inspiration.

Or you could try all of the above—and some of the ideas below:

START WITH SOME BASIC QUESTIONS

- How would you like to spend the next five or ten or twenty years?

- What community or national or global problems motivate you to act?

- How much income do you need to earn?

- Do you want to stay in the same field or explore something new?

- Do you want to start your own organization or work for an existing one?

- Are you willing and able to go back to school or get other training?

CONSIDER WHETHER YOU'D LIKE TO BE A CAREER RECYCLER, CAREER CHANGER, OR CAREER MAKER

Career recyclers build on their expertise in one field to transition to the next—like a salesperson who becomes a development director for a nonprofit organization. Or a truck driver who becomes a driver for disabled citizens. Or someone like Kaye Warren, a longtime computer specialist who launched a satisfying new career teaching computer science at a community college.

Career changers thrive on the uncertainty and excitement of starting fresh. Brigadier General Michael P. Mulqueen left the U.S. Marine Corps to take the top job at the Greater Chicago Food Depository, one of the nation's biggest hunger-relief outfits, and has attracted national attention for the ways he has improved, even revolutionized, services there. Carol Harris-Mannes gave up a long career in acting, went back to college, earned a master's degree, and became a social worker with the Actors' Fund in New York City.

Career makers figure out how to take a lifelong interest and parlay it into a job that helps others. Emily Kimball lived her dream at sixty-two—to ride her bike across the United States—then joined the lecture circuit, earning a small income speaking to older adults about the importance of being active.

Jo Manhart had a successful career working with a trade association, after which she started an employment agency in her Missouri hometown to help older workers find jobs.

THINK HARD ABOUT YOUR OWN MOTIVATIONS AND WHAT MAKES YOU HAPPY

Jeri Sedlar and Rick Miners, authors of *Don't Retire, REWIRE!* have developed a list of thirty "drivers" to help you examine your reasons for working, beyond salary. The goal is to whittle the list down to five. (Merrill Lynch includes a one-page worksheet based on Sadler and Miners's work, which can be found at http://askmerrill.ml.com/ask_merrill_2006/5_total_merrill/retirement_illustrator/envision/images/pdf/discover_your_drivers_checklist.pdf.)

If you're prepared to invest, check out My Next Phase, at http://www.mynextphase.com, which includes a range of services—from an online assessment to group tele-classes to private coaching—at a range of prices, from $39.95 to $395. *Business Week* gave this site an A.

Other online sources for assessing your skills and interests include:

- The Career Key, at http://www.careerkey.org/
  This site offers several self-evaluation surveys and resources to help you make the best possible career choice.

- Clifton StrengthsFinder, at http://www.strengthsfinder .com/
  In tandem with the book *Now Discover Your Strengths*, this site helps individuals identify their particular areas of relative strength via extensive survey methods developed by the Gallup Organization.

- The Occupational Outlook Handbook, at http://www .bls.gov/oco/
  Published by the Department of Labor, this book contains information on the training, education, earnings, and work conditions for hundreds of types of jobs.

- The Princeton Review Career Quiz, at http://www.prince tonreview.com/cte/quiz/default.asp?menuID=0&careers=6
  A survey from the renowned college preparatory organization can help you sort out your priorities.

- The Self-Directed Search, at http://www.self-directed-search.com/
  For more insight on career decisions, this site provides a survey and a detailed, personalized assessment of the fields and careers that best fit your interests.

- What Color Is Your Parachute? at http://www.jobhunters bible.com/
  Acclaimed author Richard Bolles's "Job Hunter's Bible" Web site is a clearinghouse of information, resources, and advice for "job-hunters and career-changers."

- 2Young2Retire at http://www.2young2retire.com/
  This site provides "ideas and information, courses and trainings, tips and tools" for those considering a second career.

SELL EXPERIENCE AS AN ASSET

Stress your reliability, good judgment, problem-solving ability, ability to navigate a crisis, experience in negotiating compromise, ability to listen, ability to assess cost-benefit trade-offs, comfort level in working with all types of personalities, sense of responsibility, established identity, and sense of purpose. And stress that people of different ages bring to a team different and valuable life experiences, perspectives, and ideas. You add a positive, new dimension to a diverse workforce.

EASE YOUR WAY IN

Try a few things before leaping headlong into a commitment. Perhaps you can find an internship or work part-time as a temp on an exploratory basis. Volunteer as a way to ease yourself into a paid position.

THINK ABOUT COMPENSATION IN A NEW WAY

You'll likely face trade-offs in building a new life dedicated to the greater good. Some people trade the freedom of early retirement for a job with health benefits. Others trade a high salary for the chance to work on interesting problems and the rewards of spending time doing something important. If you'd like to know more about salaries in the nonprofit world, check out these publications: *The NonProfit Times Annual Salary Survey* (http://www.nptimes.com), *Compensation in Nonprofit Organizations* by Abbott, Langer, and Associates (http://www.abbott-langer.com) and the Guidestar Compensation Report (http://www.guidestar.org).

Learn more about the nonprofit sector in general by checking out Bridgestar (http://www.bridgestar.org), Guide Star (http://www.guidestar.org), Independent Sector (http://www.independentsector.org), the *NonProfit Times* (http://www.nptimes.com), and the National Council of Nonprofit Associations (http://www.ncna.org).

LOOK FOR ENCORE CAREER IDEAS IN FIELDS THAT MOTIVATE YOU

HEALTH CARE. Many health professions are among the top job-growth areas in America, which explains why the American Hospital Association actively encourages hospitals to recruit midlife career changers.

You don't have to be a doctor or nurse to work in health care, of course. There are more than 100 other areas of specialization—from music and art therapy to occupational health and safety—all generally known as the "allied health professions."

In response to health care labor shortages, new opportunities are opening up for streamlined training, including train-while-you-work positions.

For instance, at Cozby-Germany Hospital in Grand Saline, Texas, employees are offered the opportunity to advance their skills and education when the hospital needs employees in higher-level jobs. They don't set age limits, but they do consider whether an employee will be long term. Those who make at least a two-year commitment, and live up to it, don't have to pay the hospital back for financial assistance provided in the form of loans.

There is strong demand for numerous positions that require one, two, or three years of training, including "imaging technologists" who work with X-rays, MRIs, mammograms, and other imaging diagnostics; clinical lab workers; registered nurses; medical assistants; and home-care attendants for the disabled or elderly. Health institutions also need non-clinical workers, for instance, in information technology and record keeping.

In some areas and occupations, you may be able to find part-time work at a hospital while participating in a clinical training program for a new career.

And finally, if you have worked in the health care industry

in the past, you might consider returning. In Atlanta, Emory University Hospital has established reentry programs, offering a fully paid eight-week training program for qualified employees who agree to work for the hospital for one or two years.

Resources for health care careers include:

- Occupational Outlook Handbook, at http://www.bls.gov/oco
  From the U.S. Department of Labor; includes job descriptions and other useful details about health care jobs.

- The American Medical Association (AMA), at http://www.ama.org
  Includes annual guide, *Health Professions Career and Education Directory*, plus a list of health care professional associations, salaries, and training requirements. Free monthly *Health Professions E-letter* covers educational trends and career-related issues for more than 60 health-related professions.

- Discover Nursing, at http://www.discovernursing.com
  Information on jobs and training programs in nursing.

- Health Care Workforce, at http://www.healthcareworkforce.org
  "Ideas in Action" links to dozens of innovative programs.

- American Society for Healthcare Human Resources Administration, at http://www.ashhra.org
Information on training, plus links to postings for administrative jobs in health care.

- American Association of Colleges of Nursing, at http://www.aacn.nche.edu/publications/issues/Aug02.htm
Information on acclerated programs that provide a fast track to careers in nursing.

EDUCATION. The nation is in need of educators. The shortage is most acute in cities. And everywhere, there is great need for teachers in math, sciences, and special education.

Why teach? Experienced teachers tell pollsters that the single biggest reason to teach is the pleasure of working with young people. Achieving success with young people is incredibly fulfilling. And, as someone with considerable know-how, you have the life experience to work with parents, knowing that their attitude and involvement can make a big difference in a child's education.

If you have a bachelor's degree—in any field—you could qualify for an alternative teacher preparation program that enables you to begin teaching, with salary and benefits, within a short time. But don't underestimate the need to learn more about classroom management, local curriculum requirements, and evaluation of student progress.

If you're going to make the commitment to teaching,

presumably you'd like to be able to continue this new career for a while. Research suggests that people who make mid-career transfers into teaching can benefit by getting a good preview of the job. To get a flavor for teaching, try it out first. Sign up with your local school district to become a substitute teacher. Learn as much as you can about the school community where you'd like to work—the culture, the students' backgrounds and academic profiles, what kinds of formal and informal supports exist, and how much support and supervision you're likely to receive.

In addition to full-time K–12 teaching and part-time subbing, there are other options for those interested in educating young people. There's a need for day care teachers and providers, staff members in after-school programs, classroom assistants (particularly those who are interested in working with special-education students), tutors (paid and unpaid), and adjunct professors who teach a course or two at a local university or community college. Check into options in your community.

If you'd like to tutor or mentor elementary school students, Experience Corps may be for you. Now in twenty cities, Experience Corps trains, places, and supports teams of Americans over fifty-five who work in high-needs schools, helping children learn to read.

Resources for education careers include:

• American Board for Certification of Teacher Excellence, at http://www.abcte.org/passport.html

Provides a "Passport to Teaching certification" for individuals interested in entering teaching, including retirees.

- Experience Corps, at http://www.experiencecorps.org
  For Americans over fifty-five who want to tutor and mentor kids in underserved schools. Stipends available.

- Troops to Teachers, at http://www.proudtoserveagain.com
  Funded by the Department of Defense to help military retirees enter teaching.

- National Center for Alternative Certification (1-866-778-2784 (toll free), at http://www.teachnow.org
  A clearinghouse for information about alternative routes to certification, funded by the U.S. Department of Education. For a free publication, *Alternative Routes to Teacher Certification*, go to http://www.ed.gov/admins/tchrqual.

- National Teacher Recruitment Clearinghouse, at http://www.recruitingteachers.org/channels/clearinghouse
  Resources for career-changers interested in becoming teachers.

THE AGING FIELD. Aging is a growth field. As the U.S. population ages, expect an increase in the number of organizations dedicated to helping people age well.

One-on-one work with a disabled or impaired older

individual can be tremendously rewarding. This is one realm in which your own judgment, life experience, patience, and humor can make a real difference in someone's life. Indeed, many midlife men and women who have informally provided care for a family member discover in themselves an aptitude for this kind of interpersonal care and become interested in it as a new career.

You would be right if you assumed that this area of work might entail meal preparation, shopping, making appointments, and providing transportation to and from doctor's appointments, as well as companionship and personal care. There may also be a place in the world of elder care for other kinds of contributors: storytellers, oral historians to record the memories of older folks, yoga teachers, and line dance instructors, not to mention people who can teach computer skills.

Intergenerational programs may also generate jobs for former teachers, instructional assistants, librarians, and psychologists.

Resources for aging careers include:

- Exploring Careers in Aging, at http://www.exploring careersinaging.com

- Generations United, at http://www.gu.org
  The nation's largest database of intergenerational programs.

- National Caregiving Alliance, at http://www.caregiving
.org
Resources on caregiving, information, contacts.

- Temple University Center for Intergenerational Learning, at http://www.temple.edu/cil
Resources about model intergenerational programs, volunteer opportunities, networking.

GOVERNMENT. The federal government is the nation's largest employer, with nearly 3 million employees working on behalf of the American people all over the country. Civil service jobs are available in every state, and many offer good benefits, flexible scheduling, and opportunities for advancement.

- USAJOBS, at http://www.usajobs.opm.gov/
The federal government's job site, this searchable database contains every federal job listing and allows you to submit your résumé and application online.

- Federal Jobs Net, at http://www.federaljobs.net/
This site provides a "career center" for those seeking jobs with the federal government.

- Government Jobs, at http://www.governmentjobs.com/
A comprehensive searchable database of public sector jobs is available here.

THE NONPROFIT SECTOR. If you're leaning toward work in a nonprofit organization, there are literally more than a million choices. There are about 1.8 million nonprofit organizations in the United States—and no two are exactly alike.

Start by identifying the issues you care about and the organizations that address them. Then zero in on how your experience might help advance the group's mission. Most nonprofit organizations have Web sites and list job openings online, so if you know one where you'd like to work, check there first.

And check out the following more general online job listings for those interested in nonprofit work:

- Bridgestar, at http://www.bridgestar.org
  Job listings of senior positions in nonprofit organizations.

- Charitychannel.com Career Search Online, at http://www
  .charitychannel.com
  Job listings that can be sorted by job title, organization, or location.

- Common Good Careers, at http://www.cgcareers.org/
  A nonprofit job search firm, this organization can connect you with information and placement opportunities in the sector.

- Community Career Center, at http://www.nonprofitjobs
  .org/

This "online gathering place" allows both nonprofits and individuals to post opportunities and credentials.

- ExecSearches.com, at http://www.execsearches.com
Executive, fund-raising and midlevel jobs in nonprofit, government, health care, education, and other not-for-profit sectors.

- Energize, Inc., at http://www.energizeinc.com/placements .html
Listing of jobs and internships related to volunteer management.

- Idealist.org, at http://www.idealist.org
Lists jobs and internships in nonprofit organizations, plus tips on finding work in the nonprofit sector.

- Job Finders Online, at http://www.planningcommunica tions.com/jf/index.htm
Includes listing and guidebooks on government and nonprofit jobs.

- Jobs4.0, at http://www.jobs4point0.com/
Searchable listings of job opportunities for those forty and older.

- Monster.com, in partnership with AARP, at http:// jobsearch.aarp.monster.com/

Job database searchable by location and categories of non-profit careers.

- Noacentral.org, at http://www.gadgetfarm.com/noa/job bank
  Job listings in organizations that work for social, economic, and environmental justice.

- Nonprofitjobs.org, at http://www.nonprofitjobs.org
  Searchable job openings in nonprofit organizations.

- Nonprofit Oyster, at http://www.nonprofitoyster.com
  Searchable job listings and a place to post your résumé.

- *Nonprofit Times*, at http://nptjobs.com/
  With a circulation of over 85,000, this publication allows its users to search for nonprofit jobs online.

- Opportunityknocks.org, at http://www.opportunitynocs .org
  Search for nonprofit jobs by keyword or multiple criteria.

- Philanthropy.com, at http://philanthropy.com/jobs
  Job listings primarily in foundations.

- Philanthropy News Digest Job Corner, at http://www .fdncenter.org/pnd/jobs/index.jhtml
  Openings at U.S.-based foundations, grant-making pub-

lic charities, corporate grant-making programs, and non-profit organizations.

- Retirement Jobs, at http://www.retirementjobs.com

- Senior Job Bank, at http://www.seniorjobbank.com
  Geared to help older adults find flexible, satisfying jobs.

- Social Enterprise Alliance, at http://www.se-alliance.org
  Information, contacts, events about nonprofit organizations with business ventures.

CONSIDER LAUNCHING A CAREER
AS A SOCIAL ENTREPRENEUR

What is a social entrepreneur? According to the Web site of the Skoll Foundation, "Social entrepreneurs are proven leaders whose approaches and solutions to social problems are helping to better the lives and circumstances of countless underserved or disadvantaged individuals."

Like business entrepreneurs, the Skoll Foundation continues, social entrepreneurs "tap into vast reserves of ambition, creativity and resourcefulness in relentless pursuit of hard, measurable results. But social entrepreneurs seek to grow more than just profits. Motivated by altruism and a profound desire to promote the growth of equitable civil societies, social entrepreneurs pioneer innovative, effective, sustainable approaches to meet the needs of the marginalized, the disadvantaged and the disenfranchised."

You can find out more about social entrepreneurship by checking out:

- Ashoka, at http://www.ashoka.org
  Provides fellowships to social entrepreneurs worldwide.

- How to Change the World, at http://www.howtochange theworld.org
  Showcases the book *How to Change the World: Social Entrepreneurs and the Power of New Ideas,* by David Bornstein.

- The Purpose Prize, at http://www.purposeprize.org
  Five $100,000 awards each year to social entrepreneurs over sixty.

- The Skoll Foundation, at http://www.skollfoundation.org and http://www.socialedge.org
  Comprehensive resources, including information about grants, conferences, and other social entrepreneurs.

- The Schwab Foundation for Social Entrepreneurship, at http://www.schwabfound.org
  Provides a global platform to promote social entrepreneurship as a key element to advance societies and address social problems.

- Center for the Advancement of Social Entrepreneurship, at http://www.fuqua.duke.edu/centers/case
A research and education center based at Duke University's Fuqua School of Business.

- Stanford Center for Social Innovation, at http://www .gsb.stanford.edu/csi/
Located at the Stanford Graduate School of Business. Publishes the *Stanford Social Innovation Review*.

- Social Enterprise Alliance, at http://www.se-alliance.org
An association of individuals and organizations building effective, more sustainable nonprofits through earned-income strategies.

- Kauffman Foundation, at http://www.kauffman.org
Focuses its grant making and operations on two areas: advancing entrepreneurship and improving the education of children and youth.

For more information and more resources to help you find your encore career, please visit http://www.encorecareer.org.

The following sections set out the materials I relied upon in writing *Encore*, along with selected annotations.

FIRST-PERSON NARRATIVES AND INTERVIEWS

The five first-person narratives included between the chapters of the book were distilled from many interviews conducted as part of Civic Ventures' *Still Working* project, funded by the Robert Wood Johnson Foundation and the Pamela and Pierre Omindyar Fund at the Peninsula Community Foundation. For the purpose of the book, and to enhance clarity, they were turned into narratives from interview transcripts. These interviews were conducted by me and by several others at Civic Ventures during the period 2004 through 2007.

CHAPTER I

9 *Between 2003 and 2005, workers over 55 comprised the fastest growing group.* John Challenger, "Career Pros: New Interest in Older Jobseekers," *California Job Journal*, September 24, 2006. http://www.jobjournal.com/article_printer.asp?artid=1807.

20 *In fact, the 2005 MetLife Foundation/Civic Ventures New Face of Work study.* MetLife Foundation/Civic Ventures, "New Face

of Work Survey," conducted by Princeton Survey Research Associates, June 2005.

22 *because Marge Piercy is right.* Marge Piercy, *To Be of Use: Poems by Marge Piercy* (New York: Doubleday, 1973).

23 *According to a survey conducted by AARP.* Roper ASW, "Staying Ahead of the Curve 2003: The AARP Working in Retirement Study," Washington, DC: AARP, September 2003. http://www.aarp.org/stayingahead.

24 *Demographer James Vaupel, director of the laboratory on longevity.* James W. Vaupel and Elke Loichinger, "Redistributing Work in Aging Europe," *Science,* June 30, 2006, pp. 1911–1913, as quoted in John Tierney, "The Adams Principle," *New York Times,* June 21, 2005.

CHAPTER 2

This chapter is adapted from two earlier publications: my book *Prime Time,* and an essay written for the Outlook section of the *Washington Post* in January 2006, "The Selling of Retirement and How We Bought It."

Here, as in the earlier pieces, the history of aging in America is distilled entirely from seven outstanding sources: (1) W. Andrew Achenbaum, *Old Age in a New Land;* (2) Achenbaum's *Wilson Quarterly* essay, "What Is Retirement For?"; (3) Thomas R. Cole, *The Journey of Life: A Cultural History of Aging in America;* (4) Dora Costa, *The Evolution of Retirement: An American Economic History;* (5) David J. Ekerdt, "Retirement," in George Maddox, ed., *The Encyclopedia of Aging;* (6) David Hackett Fischer, *Growing Old in America;* (7) and William Graebner, *A History of Retirement: The Meaning and Function of an American Institution, 1885–1978.*

The material on Walter Reuther comes from Nelson Lichtenstein's *The Most Dangerous Man in Detroit: Walter Reuther and the Fate of American Labor*, Malcolm Gladwell's "The Risk Pool," and Reuther's speeches and writings. The New Deal social compact and Social Security context is based on Jonathan Alter's *The Defining Moment*.

The story of Webb and Sun City derives from numerous sources: papers and advertisements housed at the Sun Cities Area Historical Society in Sun City, Arizona; information provided by the Del Webb Company (largely through its Web site); interviews with individuals living in Sun City and Sun City West; and an array of secondary sources (from which the vast majority of quotations are drawn). These sources include the following: Del Webb Corporation, "Del Webb: The Man"; Margaret Finnerty, *Del Webb: A Man, a Company*; Jane Freeman and Glenn Sanberg, *Jubilee: The 25th Anniversary of Sun City, Arizona*; "A Place in the Sun," *Time*; "Spreading Webb," *Time*; and Calvin Trillin, "Wake up and Live," the *New Yorker*.

For the implications of Sun City and the Golden Years, I drew primarily on David J. Eckerdt's work, including "The Busy Ethic: Moral Continuity Between Work and Retirement," in *Gerontologist*; Frances FitzGerald, *Cities on a Hill: A Journey Through Contemporary American Cultures*; Mike Steere, "Ready When You Are," in *Worth*, among other excellent sources.

34 *Now telegrams were arriving from autoworker locals.* "Carrying the Ball," *Time*, July 25, 1949, at http://www.time.com/time/magazine/arrticle/0,9171,853844,00.html.

39 *Historian W. Andrew Achenbaum quotes an economist.* W. Andrew Achenbaum, "What Is Retirement For?" *Wilson Quarterly* (Spring 2006), pp. 50–56.

39 *This combination of forces pushed many older workers out.* Cited in ibid.

40 *"I have worked hard all my life"*. quotes in Robin Toner, "'A Great Calamity Has Come Upon Us,'" *New York Times*, January 23, 2005.

41 *Long had signed up 7 million followers by 1935.* Jonathan Alter, *The Defining Moment: FDR's Hundred Days and the Triumph of Hope* (New York: Simon and Schuster, 2006), p. 310.

41 *Roosevelt used his confidence "to win power, restore hope"*. Ibid.

42 *The New Deal, Michael Tomasky writes.* Michael Tomasky, "Party in Search of a Notion," *American Prospect*, May 2006, at http://www.prospect.org/web/printfriendly-view.ww?id=11424.

43 *In 1940, the first Social Security check was issued.* Achenbaum, "What Is Retirement For?" p. 53.

43 *Ernest Burgess of the University of Chicago.* As quoted in Marvin B. Sussman, "1981 Burgess Address Law and Legal Systems: The Family Connection," *Journal of Marriage and the Family*, Vol. 45, No. 1 (Feb. 1983), pp. 9–21. http://links .jstor.org/.

43 *Lewis Mumford, the great social critic, lamented.* Lewis Mumford, "For Older People—Not Segregation but Integration," *Architectural Record*, May 1956.

47 *The pitch, says historian William Graebner.* William Graebner, *A History of Retirement: The Meaning and Function of an American Institution, 1885–1978* (New Haven: Yale University Press, 1980).

50 *Owen Childress, the manager responsible for sales.* See Jane Freeman and Glenn Sanberg, *Jubilee: The 25th Anniversary of Sun City, Arizona* (Sun City: The Sun City Historical Society, 1984).

53 *And a remarkable transformation it was.* In particular see John Robins and Geoffrey Godbey, *Time for Life: The Surprising Ways Americans Use their Time* (State College: Pennsylvania State University Press, 1997), and John Robinson, Perla

Werner, and Geoffrey Godbey, "Freeing up the Golden Years," *American Demographics*, October 1997.

54 *When the writer Calvin Trillin visited Sun City.* Calvin Trillin, "Wake up and Live," *New Yorker*, April 4, 1964.

55 *Sociologist David Ekerdt of the University of Kansas calls this.* See David J. Eckerdt, "The Busy Ethic: Moral Continuity Between Work and Retirement," *Gerontologist*, 1986.

CHAPTER 3

67 *"We have a Category 5 financial hurricane".* Terry Savage, "Boomer Retirement Storm Looms," *TheStreet.com*, May 25, 2006; Richard Wolff, "A 'Fiscal Hurricane' on the Horizon," *USA Today*, November 14, 2005; Nicholas Eberstadt, "The Old Age Tsunami," *Wall Street Journal*, November 15, 2005.

68 *In* The Coming Generational Storm. Laurence J. Kotlikoff, *The Coming Generational Storm: What You Need to Know About America's Economic Future* (Cambridge: MIT Press, 2005).

68 *The unmistakable sign of heavy economic weather.* Ibid. Also see Joie Chen, "Cloudy Future for Retirees," CBS News, March 21, 2004, at http://www.cbsnews.com/stories/2004/03/18/sunday/main607191.shtml.

68 Atlantic Monthly *writer Charles Mann bemoans.* Charles C. Mann, "The Coming Death Shortage," *Atlantic Monthly*, May 2005, at http://www.theatlantic.com/doc/200505/mann2.

69 *According to the United Nations, global aging.* "Aging Workforce 2006 Report," Watson Wyatt Worldwide, p. 4, at http://www.watsonwyatt.com/asiapacific/localsites/singapore/docs/Ageing Workforce_ap.pdf.

69 *As the late John Gardner . . . often said.* Conversations with the author.

70 *In 2006, the first of more than 76 million boomers.* "Age Data," U.S. Census Bureau, at http://www.census.gov/population/ www/socdemo/age.html#older.

71 *Even China . . . will have one in three people over sixty.* "Expert Suggests Postponing the Retirement Age," *ChinaDaily.com,* February 6, 2006, at http://www.chinadaily.com.cn/english/ doc/2006-02/06/content_517601.htm/.

71 *When Franklin Roosevelt signed the bill creating Social Security.* "Report of the Committee on Economic Security," January 1935, at http://www.ssa.gov/history/reports/ces/cesbasic. html; Wan He, Manisha Sengupta, Victoria A. Velkoff, and Kimberly DeBarros, "65+ in the United States: 2005," National Institute on Aging and U.S. Census Bureau, December 2005, at http://www.census.gov/prod/2006pubs/p23-209.pdf.

72 *James Vaupel of the laboratory on longevity.* As quoted in Gina Kolata, "Could We Live Forever?" *New York Times,* November 11, 2003.

72 *Researchers at Duke University's Center for Demographic Studies.* Will Saletan, "The New 65: Biology Can Solve the Social Security Debate," *Slate,* February 22, 2005, at http://www .slate.com/id/2113883/.

72 *Most individuals are no longer broken down physically.* Eugene Steuerle, Christopher Spiro, and Richard W. Johnson, "Can Americans Work Longer?" Urban Institute, August 15, 1999.

73 *Long and healthy lives are in part the dividends.* Saletan, "The New 65."

74 *Researchers at Boston College report.* Alicia H. Munnell, Anthony Webb, and Luke Delorma, "A New National Retirement Risk Index," Center for Retirement Research at Boston College, June 2006, at http://www.bc.edu/centers/crr/issues/ ib_48.pdf.

74 *Whole industries, from airlines to autos, are dumping.* "PBGC

Releases Fiscal Year 2006 Financial Results," Pension Benefit Guaranty Corporation, Washington, D.C., November 15, 2006, at http://www.pbgc.gov/media/news-archive/2006/pr 07-05.html.

74 *Only one-third of all companies . . . offer retiree health benefits today.* "Retiree Health Benefits," Employer Health Benefits 2005 Annual Survey, Henry J. Kaiser Family Foundation and Health Research and Education Trust, September 14, 2005.

74 *Alicia Munnell, director of Boston College's Center for Retirement Research, declares.* David Wessel, Ellen E. Schultz, and Laurie McGinley, "GM's Decision to Cut Pensions Accelerates Broad Corporate Shift," *Wall Street Journal,* February 8, 2006, at http://online.wsj.com/article/SB11393666696916 7992.html?mod=home_page_one_us.

74 *Many Americans are ignorant, blissfully or otherwise.* "Many Americans' Retirement Hopes Are Filled with Holes," 2006 Retirement Confidence Survey, Employee Benefits Research Institute, April 4, 2006, at http://ebri.org/pdf/PR_ 733_4Apr06_2.pdf.

75 *David Walker of the Government Accountability Office (GAO) calculates.* David Walker's presentation, "A Look at Our Future: When Baby Boomers Retire," at http://www.gao.gov/ cghome/whitehousewalker1205/index.html.

75 *Already, states' spending on Medicaid has surpassed.* Quoted in David Bank, "Apocalypse Soon," AgeofInnovation.org, December 12, 2005, at http://civicventures.typepad.com/age_of_ innovation/2005/12/apocalypse_soon.html.

76 *If most individuals work five additional years.* Barbara Butrica, Karen E. Smith, C. Eugene Steuerle, "Working for a Good Retirement," The Urban Institute, Washington, D.C., May 23, 2006.

76 *"If you were designing a system today".* Saletan, "The New 65."

77 *As many as 64 million baby boomers.* Lynn Morton, *Managing the Mature Workforce,* The Conference Board, New York, July 2005.

78 *Industries already facing skill shortages include.* The Conference Board, "America's Aging Workforce Posing New Opportunities and Challenges for Companies," September 19, 2005, at http://www.conference-board.org/utilities/press detail.cfm?press_ID=2709.

78 *Mercer, the large consulting firm, estimates.* Ed Frauenheim, "Face of the Future: The Aging Workforce," Workforce Management, October 9, 2006, at http://www.workforce.com/section/09/feature/24/55/67/index.html: "While specific industries certainly face tight labor markets because of the graying workforce, some experts say companies would be wise to tune out sky-is-falling prognostications of a widespread talent shortage."

78 *The retirement wave is exacerbating long-standing shortages.* "Nursing Facts: Nursing Shortage," American Nurses Association, at http://www.nursingworld.org/readroom/fsshortage .htm.

78 *In the nonprofit sector, the aging of senior managers.* Tom Tierney, "The Leadership Deficit," *Stanford Social Innovation Review* (Summer 2006), at http://www.ssireview.org/articles/entry/the_leadership_deficit/.

80 *Some in the new fifty-five-plus workforce.* "The Working Retired," Putnam Investments, December 8, 2005, at http://www.putnam.com/shared/pdf/press_working_retired.pdf; "Living Longer, Working Longer: The Changing Landscape of the Aging Workforce," David DeLong & Associates and Zogby International, MetLife Mature Market Institute, April 2006, at http://www.metlife.com/WPSAssets/195721911011 56517010V1FLivingLonger.pdf; "2006 Merrill Lynch New

Retirement Study," Merrill Lynch, May 18, 2006, at http://
askmerrill.ml.com/ask_merrill_2006/5_total_merrill/retire
ment_illustrator/retirement_main.asp.

81 *Social connections are a key to successful aging.* John W. Rowe and
Robert L. Kahn, *Successful Aging: The MacArthur Foundation
Study Shows You How the Lifestyle Choices You Make Now—
More Than Heredity—Determine Your Health* (New York:
Random House, 1998).

81 *Such strong social connections, a key feature of work.* Mary Ellen
Strote, "Why 'Joiners' Are Healthier," *Shape*, November 2003.

81 *A long-term study of nuns found that.* Pam Belluck, "Nuns Offer
Clues to Alzheimer's and Aging," *New York Times*, May 7,
2001.

81 *Other researchers have found that tutoring.* Linda P. Fried,
Michelle C. Carlson, Marc Freedman, et al., "A Social Model
for Health Promotion for an Aging Population: Initial Evidence on the Experience Corps Model," *Journal of Urban
Health* 81 (1) (March 2004), pp. 64–78, cited at http://www
.experiencecorps.org/research/JHU_summary.html.

82 *A study in Jerusalem of 1,000 men and women.* Tara Parker-
Pope, "Encore (A Special Report)—Health Matters: Work
May Hold One Key to a Longer Life," *Wall Street Journal*,
June 28, 2004.

82 *"There seem to be health benefits".* Emily Brandon, "Working
Can Boost Your Health, Keeping You Active and Sharp," *U.S.
News & World Report*, June 12, 2006.

83 *William James understood this.* As quoted in Andrea Taylor,
"Are We What Survives Us?" *Coming of Age*, http://www
.comingofage.org/volunteer/22; John Kotre, *Outliving the Self:
How We Live on in Future Generations* (New York: Norton,
1996).

83 *Drawing on Erikson's work . . . Vaillant positions generativity.*

George E. Vaillant, *Aging Well: Surprising Guideposts to a Happier Life from the Landmark Harvard Study of Adult Development* (Boston: Little, Brown, 2002).

83 *Of course, the boomers' search for meaningful work.* Russell Muirhead, *Just Work* (Cambridge: Harvard University Press, 2004), quoted in Daniel McGinn, "Second Time Around," *Newsweek*, June 19, 2006.

83 *A survey by Smith Barney concluded that tens of millions.* "The Dream Continues," Smith Barney, April 2006, at http://www.smithbarney.com/features/dreamcontinues.html.

CHAPTER 4

101 *a recent survey by Thrivent Lutheran Services.* "Thriving in Retirement," Thrivent Financial, October 2006, at http://www.thrivent.com/newsroom/pdf/survey_key_findings.pdf.

102 *Marty Rhodes, chairman of the name-change committee.* Cheryl Walker, "Goodbye Leisure World, Hello Laguna Woods Village," *Orange County Register,* October 13, 2005.

103 *In a recent survey of 500 sixty-year-olds.* "Bell Investment Advisors National Survey," Bell Investment, August 2006, at http://www.bellinvest.com/survey.html.

104 *In* A Fresh Map of Life . . . *Laslett challenges us.* Peter Laslett, *A Fresh Map of Life: The Emergence of the Third Age* (Cambridge: Harvard University Press, 1991).

106 *Some thoughtful commentators in America have taken up.* Abigail Trafford, *My Time: Making the Most of the Rest of Your Life* (New York: Basic Books, 2003); Suzanne Braun Levine, *Inventing the Rest of Our Lives: Women in Second Adulthood* (New York: Penguin, 2005); Gene Cohen, *The Creative Age: Awakening Human Potential in the Second Half of Life* (New

York: Harper, 2001); Phyllis Moen, "Midcourse: Navigating Retirement and a New Life Stage," in Jeylan Mortimer and Michael J. Shanahan, eds., *Handbook of the Life Course* (New York: Kluwer Publishers, 2003).

106 *Shoshana Zuboff of Harvard Business School laid out a schema.* Shoshanna Zuboff, "The New Adulthood," *Fast Company*, August 2004, at http://www.fastcompany.com/magazine/85/szuboff.html.

107 *Zuboff, like Laslett, turned to social innovation directly.* Ibid.

110 *Midlife overwork has reached pathological proportions.* Steven Greenhouse, "Report Shows Americans Have More 'Labor Days,'" *New York Times*, September 1, 2001.

111 *Putnam estimated about twice as many of the unretired.* Michael Hill, "When a retirement is not a retirement," Associated Press State and Local Wire, March 5, 2006.

111 *"A growing number of mid-career professionals".* Herminia Ibarra, *Working Identity: Unconventional Strategies for Reinventing Your Career* (Boston: Harvard Business School Press, 2002).

111 *"Adulthood simply goes on too long".* "The HBR List: Breakthrough Ideas for 2005," *Harvard Business Review* (February 2005), p. 17.

112 *Further feeding this trend is compression in the span.* Marc Galanter, "Old and In the Way: The Coming Demographic Transformation of the Legal Profession and Its Implications for the Provision of Legal Services," *Wisconsin Law Review* (1999), at http://marcgalanter.net/Documents/papers/ComingDemographicTransformation.pdf.

118 *"The boomers are healthy, they haven't saved a lot of money".* "Not Getting Older, Just More Scrutinized," *New York Times*, October 11, 2006.

118 *Perhaps the best commentary on all these strange juxtapositions.*

Melanie Joy Douglas, "Baby Boomers Just Won't Stop Working," Monster.ca, at http://content.monster.ca/12320_en-CA_p1.asp.

121 *Laslett, who called for those in the third age to create.* Laslett, *A Fresh Map of Life.*

CHAPTER 5

This chapter owes a great debt to two outstanding books, *Gig: Americans Talk About Their Jobs* and *The Collar: A Year Inside a Catholic Seminary.* The entire Jim Churchman story is drawn from *Gig*, edited by John Bowe, Marisa Bowe, and Sabin Streeter. *Gig* is a remarkable book that lets Americans reflect on their experience at work. The account of the Sacred Heart Seminary is inspired by, and draws heavily upon, Jonathan Englert's *The Collar*, a powerful account of men training for the priesthood at the Hales Corners seminary. The interview of Father Tom Knoebel was conducted by Brad Edmondson.

131 *Churchman tells his story in the book Gig.* John Bowe, Marisa Bowe, and Sabin Streeter, *Gig: Americans Talk About Their Jobs* (New York: Three Rivers Press, 2000).

132 *Joseph Quinn, professor of economics.* Kevin E. Cahill, Michael D. Giandrea, and Joseph F. Quinn, "Are Traditional Retirements a Thing of the Past? New Evidence on Retirement Patterns and Bridge Jobs," September 29, 2005, at http://aging andwork.bc.edu/documents/bridge_jobs_post_002.pdf.

134 *Study after study has shown that workers.* Kathleen Christensen, "Getting the Right Fit: Flexible Work Options and Older Workers," Center on Aging and Work, Boston College, July 18, 2005.

135 *For older women who leave the workforce.* Kathleen Christensen, "Alfred P. Sloan Foundation's National Initiative on Workplace Flexibility," Sloan Foundation, at http://141.161.16.100/workplaceflexibility2010/docs/SloanInitiative.pdf.

136 *"Most jobs are mismatched with the competencies".* Christensen, "Getting the Right Fit."

137 *"I'm sure you have probably heard".* "Seminarians Have More in Common than Vocation," Sam Lucaro, *Catholic Herald,* January 13, 2005.

138 *According to* The Collar, *Jonathan Englert's study.* Jonathan Englert, *The Collar: A Year of Striving and Faith Inside a Catholic Seminary* (Boston: Houghton Mifflin, 2006).

138 *Now, Sacred Heart moved aggressively to recruit "older men . . . ".* Ibid.

139 *Simple supply and demand is driving the focus.* Ibid.

140 *Growth in the number of second-career individuals.* "Catholic Ministry Formation Enrollments, Statistical Overview for 2005–2006," Center for Applied Research in the Apostolate, Georgetown University, Washington, D.C., April 2006, at http://cara.georgetown.edu/Over-view0506.pdf.

141 *"Our students are in their 40s".* Interview with Brad Edmundson.

143 *As Robert Egger, founder of the D.C. Central Kitchen.* Robert Egger, "Baked in Boston," from Robert Egger's *Piece of Mind,* March 13, 2006, at http://dccentralkitchen.blogspot.com/2006_03_01_archive.html.

154 *Encore career innovators are contributing to the dramatic increase.* Ewing Marion Kauffman Foundation, at http://www.kauffman.org/pdf/KIEA_national_052206.pdf.

156 *Drucker wrote as he neared his own tenth decade.* Peter Drucker, "Managing Oneself," Best of HBR, *Harvard Business Review,* January 2005.

156 *His 2004 essay, "What Makes an Effective Executive".* "The 46th

Annual McKinsey Awards, Winners 2004," *Harvard Business Online,* at http://harvardbusinessonline.hbsp.harvard.edu/b02/en/hbr/hbr_mckinsey_awards_2004.jhtml.

157 *Today, knowledge workers in particular.* Drucker, "Managing Oneself."

CHAPTER 6

This section draws significantly on collaboration with and on the work of two of my colleagues at Civic Ventures—David Bank on the Troops to Teachers program, and in particular, the Civic Ventures monograph *Troops to Teachers: A Model Pathway to a Second Tour of Duty;* and John Gomperts on policy options, including the Encore Fellows and the reverse GI Bill. Gomperts has written about these options in a variety of places, including the journal *Generations.*

167 *One of the most innovative career-transition initiatives.* Adapted from David Bank, "Troops to Teachers: A Model Pathway to a Second Tour of Duty," Civic Ventures Policy Series, January 2007, at http://www.civicventures.org/publications/policy_papers/pdfs/troops_teach.pdf.

181 *Taking all factors into consideration, one study found the implicit tax.* Barbara Butrica, Richard W. Johnson, Karen E. Smith, and C. Eugene Steuerle, "The Implicit Tax on Work at Older Ages," Urban Institute, June 2006, at http://www.urban.org/url.cfm?ID=1001021.

181 Ageism in America, *a major study.* "Ageism in America," International Longevity Center, New York, 2006, at http://www.ilcusa.org/_lib/pdf/Ageism%20in%20America%20-%20The%20ILC%20Report.pdf.

183 *A study by the Federal Reserve found that.* Joseph F. Pingle, "Social Security's Delayed Retirement Credit and the Labor Supply of Older Men," Federal Reserve Board, August 2006, at http://www.federalreserve.gov/pubs/feds/2006/20 0637/200637pap.pdf.

183 *According to the Kaiser Family Foundation, those over fifty.* "2006 Kaiser/Hewitt Retiree Health Benefits Survey," Kaiser Family Foundation, Menlo Park, CA, December 13, 2006, at http://www.kff.org/medicare/med121306pkg.cfm.

184 *The consulting firm Towers Perrin found.* "The Business Case for Workers Age 50+," AARP report, Towers Perrin, December 2005.

184 *A survey by Boston College's Center for Retirement Research.* Alicia H. Munnell, Steven A. Sass, and Mauricio Soto, "Employer Attitudes Towards Older Workers: Survey Results," Work Opportunities for Older Americans Series 3, Boston College, July 2006.

186 *In a Ford Foundation study nearly two decades ago.* Kris Fell, "Neighborly Communities," *Harvard Magazine* (New England Regional Edition) (January–February 1999), at http://www.harvardmag.com/jf99/ner.html.

192 *As Peter Capelli, a professor of management at the University of Pennsylvania's.* Peter Capelli, "Don't Fool Yourself: This Won't Be Easy for Employers," New Face of Work Survey, Civic Ventures, June 2005.

197 *According to science fiction writer William Gibson.* Robert Lenzner and Joanne Gordon, "The Messiahs of the Network," *Forbes,* March 8, 1999.

198 *As Peter Drucker famously remarked.* Cheryl Hall, "Drucker's Disciples Keep Faith," *Dallas Morning News,* May 21, 2006.

199 *In announcing this new trajectory, Gates stated.* Bill Gates, "A New Era of Technical Leadership at Microsoft," June

15, 2006, at http://www.microsoft.com/presspass/exec/billg/
speeches/2006/06-15transition.mspx.

199 *"I asked myself, 'What is it that really gives me pleasure?'"* Quoted
in Arianna Huffington, *On Becoming Fearless in Love, Work,
and Life* (New York: Little, Brown, 2006).

200 *What are we waiting for?* This phrase is drawn from and inspired by Ruth Van Demark's sermon "Waiting," delivered at
Vassar College, June 11, 2006.

APPENDIX

202 *they don't wait around.* Some of the contents of this section
have been published earlier in *The Boomers' Guide to Good
Work: An Introduction to Jobs That Make a Difference,* written
by Ellen Freudenheim and published by MetLife Foundation and Civic Ventures. Freudenheim is the author of *Looking Forward: An Optimist's Guide to Retirement* (New York:
Stewart, Tabori and Chang, 2004).

Achenbaum, W. Andrew. *Older Americans, Vital Communities: A Bold Vision for Societal Aging.* Baltimore: Johns Hopkins University Press, 2005.

Bornstein, David. *How to Change the World.* New York: Oxford University Press, 2004.

Bowe, John, Marisa Bowe, and Sabin Streeter. *Gig: Americans Talk About Their Jobs.* New York: Three Rivers Press, 2001.

Bronson, Po. *What Should I Do with My Life? The True Story of People Who Answered the Ultimate Question.* New York: Ballantine Books, 2005.

Buford, Bob. *Halftime: Changing Your Game Plan from Success to Significance.* Grand Rapids, MI: Zondervan, 1997.

Butler, Robert. *Why Survive? Growing Old in America.* Baltimore: Johns Hopkins University Press, 2002.

Civic Ventures, Metlife Foundation/Civic Ventures. New Face of Work study. San Francisco: Civic Ventures, 2005.

Cohen, Gene. *The Creative Age: Awakening Human Potential in the Second Half of Life.* New York: Harper, 2001.

_____. *The Mature Mind: The Positive Power of the Aging Brain.* New York: Basic Books, 2007.

Collins, Jim. *Good to Great and the Social Sectors: A Monograph to Accompany Good to Great.* New York: HarperCollins, 2005.

Corbett, Dave, and Richard Higgins. *Portfolio Life: The New Path to Work, Purpose, and Passion After 50.* San Francisco: Jossey-Bass, 2006.

Davidson, Sara. *Leap! What Will We Do with the Rest of Our Lives?* New York: Random House, 2007.

Dychtwald, Ken, and Daniel Kadlec. *The Power Years: A User's Guide to the Rest of Your Life.* Indianapolis: Wiley, 2006.

Dychtwald, Ken, Tamara Erikson, and Robert Morison. *Workforce Crisis: How to Beat the Coming Shortage of Skills And Talent.* Boston: Harvard Business School Press, 2006.

Eisenberg, Lee. *The Number: A Completely Different Way to Think About the Rest of Your Life.* New York: Free Press, 2006.

Ekerdt, David. "The Busy Ethic: Moral Continuity Between Work and Retirement." *Gerontologist* 26 (3) (June 1986): 239–244.

Englert, Jonathan. *The Collar.* Boston: Houghton Mifflin, 2006.

Fein, Richard. *The Baby Boomer's Guide to the New Workplace.* Lanham, MD: Taylor Trade Publishing, 2006.

Fogel, Robert William. *The Fourth Great Awakening and the Future of Egalitarianism.* Chicago: University Of Chicago Press, 2002.

Freudenheim, Ellen, *Looking Forward: An Optimist's Guide to Retirement.* New York: Stewart, Tabori and Chang, 2004.

Galenson, David. *Old Masters and Young Geniuses: The Two Life Cycles of Artistic Creativity.* Princeton: Princeton University Press, 2005.

Gardner, John. *Self-Renewal: The Individual and the Innovative Society.* New York: W. W. Norton and Company, 1995.

Gassner Otting, Laura. *Change Your Career: Transitioning to the Nonprofit Sector.* New York: Kaplan Publishing, 2007.

Gillon, Steve. *Boomer Nation: The Largest and Richest Generation Ever, and How It Changed America.* New York: Free Press, 2004.

Graebner, William. *A History of Retirement: The Meaning and Function of an American Institution, 1885–1978.* New Haven: Yale University Press, 1984.

Handy, Charles. *The Age of Unreason*. Boston: Harvard Business School Press, 1998.

Hochschild, Arlie. *The Time Bind: When Work Becomes Home and Home Becomes Work*. New York: Henry Holt and Company, 2001.

Ibarra, Herminia. *Working Identity: Unconventional Strategies for Reinventing Your Career*. Boston: Harvard Business School Press, 2004.

Kanter, Rosabeth Moss. "Back to College: Ending a Career Will Soon Mark the Start of a New Life." *AARP Magazine* (July–August 2006).

Laslett, Peter. *A Fresh Map of Life*. Great Britain: Palgrave Macmillan, 1996.

Leider, Richard, and David Shapiro. *Claiming Your Place at the Fire: Living the Second Half of Your Life on Purpose*. San Francisco: Berrett-Koehler Publishers, 2004.

Levine, Suzanne Braun. *Inventing the Rest of Our Lives: Women in Second Adulthood*. New York: Viking Adult, 2004.

Moen, Phyllis, and Patricia Roehling. *The Career Mystique: Cracks in the American Dream*. Lanham, MD: Rowman and Littlefield Publishers, 2004.

Morrow-Howell, Nancy, James Hinterlong, and Michael Sherraden. *Productive Aging*. Baltimore: Johns Hopkins University Press, 2006.

Muirhead, Russell. *Just Work*. Cambridge: Harvard University Press, 2007.

Novelli, Bill. *50+: Igniting a Revolution to Reinvent America*. New York: St. Martin's Press, 2006.

O'Toole, James. *Creating the Good Life: Applying Aristotle's Wisdom to Find Meaning and Happiness*. Emmaus, PA: Rodale Books, 2005.

Pink, Daniel. *Free Agent Nation: The Future of Working for Yourself*. New York: Warner Business Books, 2002.

Putnam, Robert D. *Bowling Alone: The Collapse and Revival of American Community*. New York: Simon and Schuster, 2001.

Putnam, Robert, Lewis Feldstein, and Donald Cohen. *Better Together: Restoring the American Community*. New York: Simon and Schuster, 2004.

Roszak, Theodore. *America the Wise: The Longevity Revolution and the True Wealth of Nations*. Boston: Houghton Mifflin Company, 1998.

Rowe, John Wallis, and Robert Kahn. *Successful Aging*. New York: Dell, 1999.

Ruffenach, Glenn, and Kelly Greene. *The Wall Street Journal. Complete Retirement Guidebook: How to Plan It, Live It and Enjoy It*. New York: Three Rivers Press, 2007.

Sedlar, Jeri, and Rick Miners. *Don't Retire, ReWire!* Royersford, PA: Alpha Publishing, 2002.

Steinhorn, Leonard. *The Greater Generation: In Defense of the Baby Boom Legacy*. New York: St. Martin's Griffin, 2007.

Stone, Howard, and Marika Stone. *Too Young to Retire: An Off-the-Road Map to the Rest of Your Life*. New York: Plume, 2004.

Terkel, Studs. *Working: People Talk About What They Do All Day and How They Feel About What They Do*. New York: New Press, 1997.

Trafford, Abigail. *My Time: Making the Most of the Bonus Decades After 50*. New York: Basic Books, 2004.

ACKNOWLEDGMENTS

I am grateful most of all to the encore career pioneers who are the inspiration for this book. They constitute a powerful force for a better world.

I owe deep debt to the members of this vanguard who gave so much time speaking to me and my colleagues at Civic Ventures. Nearly 200 individuals agreed to be part of the *Still Working* project, opening up their lives and telling their stories as they navigated their way to purpose and contribution. They constitute the backbone of this book, and I am very grateful to them—in particular, Beverly Ryder, Ed Speedling, Jacqueline Khan, Sandra Sessoms-Penny, Sally Bingham, Frank Reece, Steve Weiner, Velma Simpson, and Robert Chambers. I'd like to give special thanks to Fritz Schwarz, whose own encore career at the Brennan Center for Justice at NYU Law School sparked the idea for this book, and who generously spent time talking with me about his experiences charting a new phase of work.

Likewise, I am grateful to Ruth Van Demark, who helped me understand that finding a true calling in the second half of life required more than vision, but also resilience and a healthy dose of persistence. One of her eloquent sermons also supplied the book's closing call to action.

Immense thanks go also to my colleagues at Civic Ventures, most of all to David Bank: for his ideas, eloquence, savvy, camaraderie, and good humor at every step of the way with this project. Without him this book would not exist. I am likewise grateful to Alex Harris for his beautiful pictures of the people in *Encore*. Stefanie Weiss and John Gomperts, wonderful colleagues and friends, contributed mightily to this project, as did many others at Civic Ventures, including: Jim Emerman, Phyllis Segal, Judy Goggin, Doug Braley, Michelle Hynes, David Cohen, Elizabeth Fox, Marina Krutchinsky, Pat Higgins, Emily Gillingham, Richard Smith, Evelyn Ostergren, and Deborah Dalfen.

Particular thanks go to Susan Tomaro, Jenny Griffin, and John Doxey who led the *Still Working* project that produced most of the stories in this book. I'd also like to express my gratitude to Ellen Freudenheim, author of *The Boomers Guide to Good Work,* the primary source for this book's appendix. And to Jeremy Cluchey, who played an extremely important role in shepherding this book to completion. Brad Edmondson lent his research acumen at a critical juncture in this project.

Thanks go to Civic Ventures' board as well, for all their support of this project and for their many substantive contributions to it, especially to Ruth Wooden, who counseled me to think about the unfolding phenomenon not only as a new stage of life but as "a new stage of work." Sherry Lansing is a source of inspiration through her leadership of the broader movement this book describes. Former Civic Ventures' board member Phyllis Moen's groundbreaking research formed a foundation for this project, as did many conversations with our emeritus chair, Gary Walker, and current vice-chair, Mike Bailin—mentors both in life and work. I am grateful for the ongoing guidance of board members, current and past, Rex Adams, Bill Berkeley, Ann Bowers, Lew Feldstein, Jim Gibbs, John Rother, and Kelvin Taketa.

As always, I owe immense gratitude to Atlantic Philanthropies, especially to Brian Hofland and Laura Robbins. Essential support for this project and the work behind it came also from the MetLife Foundation, The Robert Wood Johnson Foundation, the David and Lucile Packard Foundation, the Skoll Foundation, The John Templeton Foundation, and the Pamela and Pierre Omidyar Fund at the Peninsula Community Foundation. Fellowships from Ashoka and the Hunt Alternatives Fund helped me get the time to develop ideas that found their way into this book.

I benefited greatly from the counsel and ideas of Andy Achenbaum, Richard Adler, Parker Blackman, David Bornstein, Jeff Bradach, Ben Brown, Laura Brown, Bob Buford, Donna Butts, Peter Capelli, Laura Carstensen, Roger Cohn, Barbara Dillon, Bill Drayton, Emily Dulcan, Tom Endres, Andy Goodman, Kelly Greene, Jacob Harold, Nancy Henkin, Jan Hively, Arlie Hochschild, Don Howard, Sibyl Jacobson, Rosabeth Moss Kanter, Carol Larson, Stan Litow, Jane Isaacs Lowe, Margaret Mark, Joe Marx, Debra Meyerson, Harry R. Moody, Mario Morino, Nancy Morrow-Howell, David Morse, Jessica Nusbaum, Daniel Pink,

Robert Putnam, Jack Rosenthal, Glenn Ruffenach, Kimon Sargent, David Simms, Mike Smith, Max Stier, Howard and Marika Stone, Herb Sturz, Tom Tierney, Bob Tobin, Abbie Trafford, Mark Valentine, Jehan Velji, Cathy Ventura-Merkel, Steve and Patricia Weiner, and many others who gave generously of their time and insights.

At PublicAffairs, I owe thanks to the entire team. Peter Osnos has been a wise mentor and keen critic through two books. His own work—creating, first, PublicAffairs and now the Caravan project, after extraordinary careers at both the *Washington Post* and Times Books—serves as a compelling example of an encore career done right. Robert Kimzey, editor extraordinaire, guided me through *Prime Time* and shepherded this book from conception to completion. I am grateful also to Susan Weinberg, Whitney Peeling, Lizzy Mason, Laura Stine, and the rest of the PublicAffairs family.

As always, John Gardner was a primary source of inspiration for this project, despite passing away in 2002. His own life served as a reminder of the possibilities of the second half of life. Awarded the Presidential Medal of Freedom—that ultimate lifetime achievement award—in 1964, already in his fifties, he seemed poised for a graceful exit. Instead, he produced decade after decade of his best work, profoundly shaping American society for the better. He was a great friend, incomparably wise, and he is deeply missed.

My greatest appreciation of all goes to Leslie Gray, my wife, who survived the book-writing process with her patience stretched but her humor, warmth, and indomitable spirit intact. I am eternally grateful for her love and support.

ABOUT THE AUTHOR AND PHOTOGRAPHER

Marc Freedman is founder and CEO of Civic Ventures. A former visiting research fellow of King's College, University of London, a frequent commentator in the national media, and the author of both *Prime Time* and *The Kindness of Strangers*, Freedman spearheaded the creation of Experience Corps and The Purpose Prize. An Ashoka Senior Fellow, he was recognized in 2007 and again in 2008 by *Fast Company* magazine as one of the nation's leading social entrepreneurs. He is based in San Francisco.

Photographer **Alex Harris** traveled across the country to make the portraits in *Encore*. A 1991 finalist for the Pulitzer Prize in nonfiction, he is the author of many books including *River of Traps* and *The Idea of Cuba*. Harris is currently Professor of the Practice of Public Policy at Duke University, where he founded the Center for Documentary Photography. Harris also cofounded *DoubleTake* magazine. He lives in Durham, North Carolina.

For more information, go to www.encore.org or
www.civicventures.org.